C-3455

CAREER EXAMINATION SERIES

THIS IS YOUR **PASSBOOK**® FOR ...

INFORMATION PROCESSING SPECIALIST

NLC®

NATIONAL LEARNING CORPORATION®
passbooks.com

COPYRIGHT NOTICE

This book is SOLELY intended for, is sold ONLY to, and its use is RESTRICTED to individual, bona fide applicants or candidates who qualify by virtue of having seriously filed applications for appropriate license, certificate, professional and/or promotional advancement, higher school matriculation, scholarship, or other legitimate requirements of educational and/or governmental authorities.

This book is NOT intended for use, class instruction, tutoring, training, duplication, copying, reprinting, excerption, or adaptation, etc., by:

1) Other publishers
2) Proprietors and/or Instructors of «Coaching» and/or Preparatory Courses
3) Personnel and/or Training Divisions of commercial, industrial, and governmental organizations
4) Schools, colleges, or universities and/or their departments and staffs, including teachers and other personnel
5) Testing Agencies or Bureaus
6) Study groups which seek by the purchase of a single volume to copy and/or duplicate and/or adapt this material for use by the group as a whole without having purchased individual volumes for each of the members of the group
7) Et al.

Such persons would be in violation of appropriate Federal and State statutes.

PROVISION OF LICENSING AGREEMENTS. — Recognized educational, commercial, industrial, and governmental institutions and organizations, and others legitimately engaged in educational pursuits, including training, testing, and measurement activities, may address request for a licensing agreement to the copyright owners, who will determine whether, and under what conditions, including fees and charges, the materials in this book may be used them. In other words, a licensing facility exists for the legitimate use of the material in this book on other than an individual basis. However, it is asseverated and affirmed here that the material in this book CANNOT be used without the receipt of the express permission of such a licensing agreement from the Publishers. Inquiries re licensing should be addressed to the company, attention rights and permissions department.

All rights reserved, including the right of reproduction in whole or in part, in any form or by any means, electronic or mechanical, including photocopying, recording, or by any information storage and retrieval system, without permission in writing from the Publisher.

Copyright © 2020 by

NLC®

National Learning Corporation

212 Michael Drive, Syosset, NY 11791
(516) 921-8888 • www.passbooks.com
E-mail: info@passbooks.com

PUBLISHED IN THE UNITED STATES OF AMERICA

PASSBOOK® SERIES

THE *PASSBOOK® SERIES* has been created to prepare applicants and candidates for the ultimate academic battlefield – the examination room.

At some time in our lives, each and every one of us may be required to take an examination – for validation, matriculation, admission, qualification, registration, certification, or licensure.

Based on the assumption that every applicant or candidate has met the basic formal educational standards, has taken the required number of courses, and read the necessary texts, the *PASSBOOK® SERIES* furnishes the one special preparation which may assure passing with confidence, instead of failing with insecurity. Examination questions – together with answers – are furnished as the basic vehicle for study so that the mysteries of the examination and its compounding difficulties may be eliminated or diminished by a sure method.

This book is meant to help you pass your examination provided that you qualify and are serious in your objective.

The entire field is reviewed through the huge store of content information which is succinctly presented through a provocative and challenging approach – the question-and-answer method.

A climate of success is established by furnishing the correct answers at the end of each test.

You soon learn to recognize types of questions, forms of questions, and patterns of questioning. You may even begin to anticipate expected outcomes.

You perceive that many questions are repeated or adapted so that you can gain acute insights, which may enable you to score many sure points.

You learn how to confront new questions, or types of questions, and to attack them confidently and work out the correct answers.

You note objectives and emphases, and recognize pitfalls and dangers, so that you may make positive educational adjustments.

Moreover, you are kept fully informed in relation to new concepts, methods, practices, and directions in the field.

You discover that you arre actually taking the examination all the time: you are preparing for the examination by "taking" an examination, not by reading extraneous and/or supererogatory textbooks.

In short, this PASSBOOK®, used directedly, should be an important factor in helping you to pass your test.

INFORMATION PROCESSING SPECIALIST

DUTIES
Operates word processing equipment with a storage medium; retrieves typed material in order to rearrange, edit, make additions, and/or to print from memory; formats work to specifications of the author; and designs parameters for selective information storage.

SUBJECT OF EXAMINATION
Written test will cover knowledge, skills, and/or abilities in such areas as:
1. Keyboarding practices.
2. Understanding and interpreting written material;
3. Spelling;
4. English grammar and usage; punctuation; and
5. Office record keeping.

HOW TO TAKE A TEST

I. YOU MUST PASS AN EXAMINATION

A. WHAT EVERY CANDIDATE SHOULD KNOW

Examination applicants often ask us for help in preparing for the written test. What can I study in advance? What kinds of questions will be asked? How will the test be given? How will the papers be graded?

As an applicant for a civil service examination, you may be wondering about some of these things. Our purpose here is to suggest effective methods of advance study and to describe civil service examinations.

Your chances for success on this examination can be increased if you know how to prepare. Those "pre-examination jitters" can be reduced if you know what to expect. You can even experience an adventure in good citizenship if you know why civil service exams are given.

B. WHY ARE CIVIL SERVICE EXAMINATIONS GIVEN?

Civil service examinations are important to you in two ways. As a citizen, you want public jobs filled by employees who know how to do their work. As a job seeker, you want a fair chance to compete for that job on an equal footing with other candidates. The best-known means of accomplishing this two-fold goal is the competitive examination.

Exams are widely publicized throughout the nation. They may be administered for jobs in federal, state, city, municipal, town or village governments or agencies.

Any citizen may apply, with some limitations, such as the age or residence of applicants. Your experience and education may be reviewed to see whether you meet the requirements for the particular examination. When these requirements exist, they are reasonable and applied consistently to all applicants. Thus, a competitive examination may cause you some uneasiness now, but it is your privilege and safeguard.

C. HOW ARE CIVIL SERVICE EXAMS DEVELOPED?

Examinations are carefully written by trained technicians who are specialists in the field known as "psychological measurement," in consultation with recognized authorities in the field of work that the test will cover. These experts recommend the subject matter areas or skills to be tested; only those knowledges or skills important to your success on the job are included. The most reliable books and source materials available are used as references. Together, the experts and technicians judge the difficulty level of the questions.

Test technicians know how to phrase questions so that the problem is clearly stated. Their ethics do not permit "trick" or "catch" questions. Questions may have been tried out on sample groups, or subjected to statistical analysis, to determine their usefulness.

Written tests are often used in combination with performance tests, ratings of training and experience, and oral interviews. All of these measures combine to form the best-known means of finding the right person for the right job.

II. HOW TO PASS THE WRITTEN TEST

A. NATURE OF THE EXAMINATION

To prepare intelligently for civil service examinations, you should know how they differ from school examinations you have taken. In school you were assigned certain definite pages to read or subjects to cover. The examination questions were quite detailed and usually emphasized memory. Civil service exams, on the other hand, try to discover your present ability to perform the duties of a position, plus your potentiality to learn these duties. In other words, a civil service exam attempts to predict how successful you will be. Questions cover such a broad area that they cannot be as minute and detailed as school exam questions.

In the public service similar kinds of work, or positions, are grouped together in one "class." This process is known as *position-classification*. All the positions in a class are paid according to the salary range for that class. One class title covers all of these positions, and they are all tested by the same examination.

B. FOUR BASIC STEPS

1) Study the announcement

How, then, can you know what subjects to study? Our best answer is: "Learn as much as possible about the class of positions for which you've applied." The exam will test the knowledge, skills and abilities needed to do the work.

Your most valuable source of information about the position you want is the official exam announcement. This announcement lists the training and experience qualifications. Check these standards and apply only if you come reasonably close to meeting them.

The brief description of the position in the examination announcement offers some clues to the subjects which will be tested. Think about the job itself. Review the duties in your mind. Can you perform them, or are there some in which you are rusty? Fill in the blank spots in your preparation.

Many jurisdictions preview the written test in the exam announcement by including a section called "Knowledge and Abilities Required," "Scope of the Examination," or some similar heading. Here you will find out specifically what fields will be tested.

2) Review your own background

Once you learn in general what the position is all about, and what you need to know to do the work, ask yourself which subjects you already know fairly well and which need improvement. You may wonder whether to concentrate on improving your strong areas or on building some background in your fields of weakness. When the announcement has specified "some knowledge" or "considerable knowledge," or has used adjectives like "beginning principles of..." or "advanced ... methods," you can get a clue as to the number and difficulty of questions to be asked in any given field. More questions, and hence broader coverage, would be included for those subjects which are more important in the work. Now weigh your strengths and weaknesses against the job requirements and prepare accordingly.

3) Determine the level of the position

Another way to tell how intensively you should prepare is to understand the level of the job for which you are applying. Is it the entering level? In other words, is this the position in which beginners in a field of work are hired? Or is it an intermediate or advanced level? Sometimes this is indicated by such words as "Junior" or "Senior" in the class title. Other jurisdictions use Roman numerals to designate the level – Clerk I, Clerk II, for example. The word "Supervisor" sometimes appears in the title. If the level is not indicated by the title, check the description of duties. Will you be working under very close supervision, or will you have responsibility for independent decisions in this work?

4) Choose appropriate study materials

Now that you know the subjects to be examined and the relative amount of each subject to be covered, you can choose suitable study materials. For beginning level jobs, or even advanced ones, if you have a pronounced weakness in some aspect of your training, read a modern, standard textbook in that field. Be sure it is up to date and has general coverage. Such books are normally available at your library, and the librarian will be glad to help you locate one. For entry-level positions, questions of appropriate difficulty are chosen – neither highly advanced questions, nor those too simple. Such questions require careful thought but not advanced training.

If the position for which you are applying is technical or advanced, you will read more advanced, specialized material. If you are already familiar with the basic principles of your field, elementary textbooks would waste your time. Concentrate on advanced textbooks and technical periodicals. Think through the concepts and review difficult problems in your field.

These are all general sources. You can get more ideas on your own initiative, following these leads. For example, training manuals and publications of the government agency which employs workers in your field can be useful, particularly for technical and professional positions. A letter or visit to the government department involved may result in more specific study suggestions, and certainly will provide you with a more definite idea of the exact nature of the position you are seeking.

III. KINDS OF TESTS

Tests are used for purposes other than measuring knowledge and ability to perform specified duties. For some positions, it is equally important to test ability to make adjustments to new situations or to profit from training. In others, basic mental abilities not dependent on information are essential. Questions which test these things may not appear as pertinent to the duties of the position as those which test for knowledge and information. Yet they are often highly important parts of a fair examination. For very general questions, it is almost impossible to help you direct your study efforts. What we can do is to point out some of the more common of these general abilities needed in public service positions and describe some typical questions.

1) General information

Broad, general information has been found useful for predicting job success in some kinds of work. This is tested in a variety of ways, from vocabulary lists to questions about current events. Basic background in some field of work, such as sociology or economics, may be sampled in a group of questions. Often these are principles which have become familiar to most persons through exposure rather than through formal training. It is difficult to advise you how to study for these questions; being alert to the world around you is our best suggestion.

2) Verbal ability

An example of an ability needed in many positions is verbal or language ability. Verbal ability is, in brief, the ability to use and understand words. Vocabulary and grammar tests are typical measures of this ability. Reading comprehension or paragraph interpretation questions are common in many kinds of civil service tests. You are given a paragraph of written material and asked to find its central meaning.

3) Numerical ability

Number skills can be tested by the familiar arithmetic problem, by checking paired lists of numbers to see which are alike and which are different, or by interpreting charts and graphs. In the latter test, a graph may be printed in the test booklet which you are asked to use as the basis for answering questions.

4) Observation

A popular test for law-enforcement positions is the observation test. A picture is shown to you for several minutes, then taken away. Questions about the picture test your ability to observe both details and larger elements.

5) Following directions

In many positions in the public service, the employee must be able to carry out written instructions dependably and accurately. You may be given a chart with several columns, each column listing a variety of information. The questions require you to carry out directions involving the information given in the chart.

6) Skills and aptitudes

Performance tests effectively measure some manual skills and aptitudes. When the skill is one in which you are trained, such as typing or shorthand, you can practice. These tests are often very much like those given in business school or high school courses. For many of the other skills and aptitudes, however, no short-time preparation can be made. Skills and abilities natural to you or that you have developed throughout your lifetime are being tested.

Many of the general questions just described provide all the data needed to answer the questions and ask you to use your reasoning ability to find the answers. Your best preparation for these tests, as well as for tests of facts and ideas, is to be at your physical and mental best. You, no doubt, have your own methods of getting into an exam-taking mood and keeping "in shape." The next section lists some ideas on this subject.

IV. KINDS OF QUESTIONS

Only rarely is the "essay" question, which you answer in narrative form, used in civil service tests. Civil service tests are usually of the short-answer type. Full instructions for answering these questions will be given to you at the examination. But in case this is your first experience with short-answer questions and separate answer sheets, here is what you need to know:

1) Multiple-choice Questions

Most popular of the short-answer questions is the "multiple choice" or "best answer" question. It can be used, for example, to test for factual knowledge, ability to solve problems or judgment in meeting situations found at work.

A multiple-choice question is normally one of three types—
- It can begin with an incomplete statement followed by several possible endings. You are to find the one ending which *best* completes the statement, although some of the others may not be entirely wrong.
- It can also be a complete statement in the form of a question which is answered by choosing one of the statements listed.
- It can be in the form of a problem – again you select the best answer.

Here is an example of a multiple-choice question with a discussion which should give you some clues as to the method for choosing the right answer:

When an employee has a complaint about his assignment, the action which will *best* help him overcome his difficulty is to
   A. discuss his difficulty with his coworkers
   B. take the problem to the head of the organization
   C. take the problem to the person who gave him the assignment
   D. say nothing to anyone about his complaint

In answering this question, you should study each of the choices to find which is best. Consider choice "A" – Certainly an employee may discuss his complaint with fellow employees, but no change or improvement can result, and the complaint remains unresolved. Choice "B" is a poor choice since the head of the organization probably does not know what assignment you have been given, and taking your problem to him is known as "going over the head" of the supervisor. The supervisor, or person who made the assignment, is the person who can clarify it or correct any injustice. Choice "C" is, therefore, correct. To say nothing, as in choice "D," is unwise. Supervisors have and interest in knowing the problems employees are facing, and the employee is seeking a solution to his problem.

2) True/False Questions

The "true/false" or "right/wrong" form of question is sometimes used. Here a complete statement is given. Your job is to decide whether the statement is right or wrong.

SAMPLE: A roaming cell-phone call to a nearby city costs less than a non-roaming call to a distant city.

This statement is wrong, or false, since roaming calls are more expensive.

This is not a complete list of all possible question forms, although most of the others are variations of these common types. You will always get complete directions for answering questions. Be sure you understand *how* to mark your answers – ask questions until you do.

V. RECORDING YOUR ANSWERS

Computer terminals are used more and more today for many different kinds of exams.

For an examination with very few applicants, you may be told to record your answers in the test booklet itself. Separate answer sheets are much more common. If this separate answer sheet is to be scored by machine – and this is often the case – it is highly important that you mark your answers correctly in order to get credit.

An electronic scoring machine is often used in civil service offices because of the speed with which papers can be scored. Machine-scored answer sheets must be marked with a pencil, which will be given to you. This pencil has a high graphite content which responds to the electronic scoring machine. As a matter of fact, stray dots may register as answers, so do not let your pencil rest on the answer sheet while you are pondering the correct answer. Also, if your pencil lead breaks or is otherwise defective, ask for another.

Since the answer sheet will be dropped in a slot in the scoring machine, be careful not to bend the corners or get the paper crumpled.

The answer sheet normally has five vertical columns of numbers, with 30 numbers to a column. These numbers correspond to the question numbers in your test booklet. After each number, going across the page are four or five pairs of dotted lines. These short dotted lines have small letters or numbers above them. The first two pairs may also have a "T" or "F" above the letters. This indicates that the first two pairs only are to be used if the questions are of the true-false type. If the questions are multiple choice, disregard the "T" and "F" and pay attention only to the small letters or numbers.

Answer your questions in the manner of the sample that follows:

32. The largest city in the United States is
    A. Washington, D.C.
    B. New York City
    C. Chicago
    D. Detroit
    E. San Francisco

1) Choose the answer you think is best. (New York City is the largest, so "B" is correct.)
2) Find the row of dotted lines numbered the same as the question you are answering. (Find row number 32)
3) Find the pair of dotted lines corresponding to the answer. (Find the pair of lines under the mark "B.")
4) Make a solid black mark between the dotted lines.

VI. BEFORE THE TEST

Common sense will help you find procedures to follow to get ready for an examination. Too many of us, however, overlook these sensible measures. Indeed, nervousness and fatigue have been found to be the most serious reasons why applicants fail to do their best on civil service tests. Here is a list of reminders:

- Begin your preparation early – Don't wait until the last minute to go scurrying around for books and materials or to find out what the position is all about.
- Prepare continuously – An hour a night for a week is better than an all-night cram session. This has been definitely established. What is more, a night a week for a month will return better dividends than crowding your study into a shorter period of time.
- Locate the place of the exam – You have been sent a notice telling you when and where to report for the examination. If the location is in a different town or otherwise unfamiliar to you, it would be well to inquire the best route and learn something about the building.
- Relax the night before the test – Allow your mind to rest. Do not study at all that night. Plan some mild recreation or diversion; then go to bed early and get a good night's sleep.
- Get up early enough to make a leisurely trip to the place for the test – This way unforeseen events, traffic snarls, unfamiliar buildings, etc. will not upset you.
- Dress comfortably – A written test is not a fashion show. You will be known by number and not by name, so wear something comfortable.
- Leave excess paraphernalia at home – Shopping bags and odd bundles will get in your way. You need bring only the items mentioned in the official notice you received; usually everything you need is provided. Do not bring reference books to the exam. They will only confuse those last minutes and be taken away from you when in the test room.
- Arrive somewhat ahead of time – If because of transportation schedules you must get there very early, bring a newspaper or magazine to take your mind off yourself while waiting.
- Locate the examination room – When you have found the proper room, you will be directed to the seat or part of the room where you will sit. Sometimes you are given a sheet of instructions to read while you are waiting. Do not fill out any forms until you are told to do so; just read them and be prepared.
- Relax and prepare to listen to the instructions
- If you have any physical problem that may keep you from doing your best, be sure to tell the test administrator. If you are sick or in poor health, you really cannot do your best on the exam. You can come back and take the test some other time.

VII. AT THE TEST

The day of the test is here and you have the test booklet in your hand. The temptation to get going is very strong. Caution! There is more to success than knowing the right answers. You must know how to identify your papers and understand variations in the type of short-answer question used in this particular examination. Follow these suggestions for maximum results from your efforts:

1) Cooperate with the monitor

The test administrator has a duty to create a situation in which you can be as much at ease as possible. He will give instructions, tell you when to begin, check to see that you are marking your answer sheet correctly, and so on. He is not there to guard you, although he will see that your competitors do not take unfair advantage. He wants to help you do your best.

2) Listen to all instructions

Don't jump the gun! Wait until you understand all directions. In most civil service tests you get more time than you need to answer the questions. So don't be in a hurry. Read each word of instructions until you clearly understand the meaning. Study the examples, listen to all announcements and follow directions. Ask questions if you do not understand what to do.

3) Identify your papers

Civil service exams are usually identified by number only. You will be assigned a number; you must not put your name on your test papers. Be sure to copy your number correctly. Since more than one exam may be given, copy your exact examination title.

4) Plan your time

Unless you are told that a test is a "speed" or "rate of work" test, speed itself is usually not important. Time enough to answer all the questions will be provided, but this does not mean that you have all day. An overall time limit has been set. Divide the total time (in minutes) by the number of questions to determine the approximate time you have for each question.

5) Do not linger over difficult questions

If you come across a difficult question, mark it with a paper clip (useful to have along) and come back to it when you have been through the booklet. One caution if you do this – be sure to skip a number on your answer sheet as well. Check often to be sure that you have not lost your place and that you are marking in the row numbered the same as the question you are answering.

6) Read the questions

Be sure you know what the question asks! Many capable people are unsuccessful because they failed to *read* the questions correctly.

7) Answer all questions

Unless you have been instructed that a penalty will be deducted for incorrect answers, it is better to guess than to omit a question.

8) Speed tests

It is often better NOT to guess on speed tests. It has been found that on timed tests people are tempted to spend the last few seconds before time is called in marking answers at random – without even reading them – in the hope of picking up a few extra points. To discourage this practice, the instructions may warn you that your score will be "corrected" for guessing. That is, a penalty will be applied. The incorrect answers will be deducted from the correct ones, or some other penalty formula will be used.

9) Review your answers
If you finish before time is called, go back to the questions you guessed or omitted to give them further thought. Review other answers if you have time.

10) Return your test materials
If you are ready to leave before others have finished or time is called, take ALL your materials to the monitor and leave quietly. Never take any test material with you. The monitor can discover whose papers are not complete, and taking a test booklet may be grounds for disqualification.

VIII. EXAMINATION TECHNIQUES

1) Read the general instructions carefully. These are usually printed on the first page of the exam booklet. As a rule, these instructions refer to the timing of the examination; the fact that you should not start work until the signal and must stop work at a signal, etc. If there are any *special* instructions, such as a choice of questions to be answered, make sure that you note this instruction carefully.

2) When you are ready to start work on the examination, that is as soon as the signal has been given, read the instructions to each question booklet, underline any key words or phrases, such as *least, best, outline, describe* and the like. In this way you will tend to answer as requested rather than discover on reviewing your paper that you *listed without describing*, that you selected the *worst* choice rather than the *best* choice, etc.

3) If the examination is of the objective or multiple-choice type – that is, each question will also give a series of possible answers: A, B, C or D, and you are called upon to select the best answer and write the letter next to that answer on your answer paper – it is advisable to start answering each question in turn. There may be anywhere from 50 to 100 such questions in the three or four hours allotted and you can see how much time would be taken if you read through all the questions before beginning to answer any. Furthermore, if you come across a question or group of questions which you know would be difficult to answer, it would undoubtedly affect your handling of all the other questions.

4) If the examination is of the essay type and contains but a few questions, it is a moot point as to whether you should read all the questions before starting to answer any one. Of course, if you are given a choice – say five out of seven and the like – then it is essential to read all the questions so you can eliminate the two that are most difficult. If, however, you are asked to answer all the questions, there may be danger in trying to answer the easiest one first because you may find that you will spend too much time on it. The best technique is to answer the first question, then proceed to the second, etc.

5) Time your answers. Before the exam begins, write down the time it started, then add the time allowed for the examination and write down the time it must be completed, then divide the time available somewhat as follows:

- If 3-1/2 hours are allowed, that would be 210 minutes. If you have 80 objective-type questions, that would be an average of 2-1/2 minutes per question. Allow yourself no more than 2 minutes per question, or a total of 160 minutes, which will permit about 50 minutes to review.
- If for the time allotment of 210 minutes there are 7 essay questions to answer, that would average about 30 minutes a question. Give yourself only 25 minutes per question so that you have about 35 minutes to review.

6) The most important instruction is to *read each question* and make sure you know what is wanted. The second most important instruction is to *time yourself properly* so that you answer every question. The third most important instruction is to *answer every question.* Guess if you have to but include something for each question. Remember that you will receive no credit for a blank and will probably receive some credit if you write something in answer to an essay question. If you guess a letter – say "B" for a multiple-choice question – you may have guessed right. If you leave a blank as an answer to a multiple-choice question, the examiners may respect your feelings but it will not add a point to your score. Some exams may penalize you for wrong answers, so in such cases *only*, you may not want to guess unless you have some basis for your answer.

7) Suggestions
   a. Objective-type questions
      1. Examine the question booklet for proper sequence of pages and questions
      2. Read all instructions carefully
      3. Skip any question which seems too difficult; return to it after all other questions have been answered
      4. Apportion your time properly; do not spend too much time on any single question or group of questions
      5. Note and underline key words – *all, most, fewest, least, best, worst, same, opposite,* etc.
      6. Pay particular attention to negatives
      7. Note unusual option, e.g., unduly long, short, complex, different or similar in content to the body of the question
      8. Observe the use of "hedging" words – *probably, may, most likely,* etc.
      9. Make sure that your answer is put next to the same number as the question
      10. Do not second-guess unless you have good reason to believe the second answer is definitely more correct
      11. Cross out original answer if you decide another answer is more accurate; do not erase until you are ready to hand your paper in
      12. Answer all questions; guess unless instructed otherwise
      13. Leave time for review

   b. Essay questions
      1. Read each question carefully
      2. Determine exactly what is wanted. Underline key words or phrases.
      3. Decide on outline or paragraph answer

4. Include many different points and elements unless asked to develop any one or two points or elements
5. Show impartiality by giving pros and cons unless directed to select one side only
6. Make and write down any assumptions you find necessary to answer the questions
7. Watch your English, grammar, punctuation and choice of words
8. Time your answers; don't crowd material

8) Answering the essay question

Most essay questions can be answered by framing the specific response around several key words or ideas. Here are a few such key words or ideas:

M's: manpower, materials, methods, money, management
P's: purpose, program, policy, plan, procedure, practice, problems, pitfalls, personnel, public relations

  a. Six basic steps in handling problems:
    1. Preliminary plan and background development
    2. Collect information, data and facts
    3. Analyze and interpret information, data and facts
    4. Analyze and develop solutions as well as make recommendations
    5. Prepare report and sell recommendations
    6. Install recommendations and follow up effectiveness

  b. Pitfalls to avoid
    1. *Taking things for granted* – A statement of the situation does not necessarily imply that each of the elements is necessarily true; for example, a complaint may be invalid and biased so that all that can be taken for granted is that a complaint has been registered
    2. *Considering only one side of a situation* – Wherever possible, indicate several alternatives and then point out the reasons you selected the best one
    3. *Failing to indicate follow up* – Whenever your answer indicates action on your part, make certain that you will take proper follow-up action to see how successful your recommendations, procedures or actions turn out to be
    4. *Taking too long in answering any single question* – Remember to time your answers properly

IX. AFTER THE TEST

Scoring procedures differ in detail among civil service jurisdictions although the general principles are the same. Whether the papers are hand-scored or graded by machine we have described, they are nearly always graded by number. That is, the person who marks the paper knows only the number – never the name – of the applicant. Not until all the papers have been graded will they be matched with names. If other tests, such as training and experience or oral interview ratings have been given, scores will be combined. Different parts of the examination usually have different weights. For example, the written test might count 60 percent of the final grade, and a rating of training and experience 40 percent. In many jurisdictions, veterans will have a certain number of points added to their grades.

After the final grade has been determined, the names are placed in grade order and an eligible list is established. There are various methods for resolving ties between those who get the same final grade – probably the most common is to place first the name of the person whose application was received first. Job offers are made from the eligible list in the order the names appear on it. You will be notified of your grade and your rank as soon as all these computations have been made. This will be done as rapidly as possible.

People who are found to meet the requirements in the announcement are called "eligibles." Their names are put on a list of eligible candidates. An eligible's chances of getting a job depend on how high he stands on this list and how fast agencies are filling jobs from the list.

When a job is to be filled from a list of eligibles, the agency asks for the names of people on the list of eligibles for that job. When the civil service commission receives this request, it sends to the agency the names of the three people highest on this list. Or, if the job to be filled has specialized requirements, the office sends the agency the names of the top three persons who meet these requirements from the general list.

The appointing officer makes a choice from among the three people whose names were sent to him. If the selected person accepts the appointment, the names of the others are put back on the list to be considered for future openings.

That is the rule in hiring from all kinds of eligible lists, whether they are for typist, carpenter, chemist, or something else. For every vacancy, the appointing officer has his choice of any one of the top three eligibles on the list. This explains why the person whose name is on top of the list sometimes does not get an appointment when some of the persons lower on the list do. If the appointing officer chooses the second or third eligible, the No. 1 eligible does not get a job at once, but stays on the list until he is appointed or the list is terminated.

X. HOW TO PASS THE INTERVIEW TEST

The examination for which you applied requires an oral interview test. You have already taken the written test and you are now being called for the interview test – the final part of the formal examination.

You may think that it is not possible to prepare for an interview test and that there are no procedures to follow during an interview. Our purpose is to point out some things you can do in advance that will help you and some good rules to follow and pitfalls to avoid while you are being interviewed.

What is an interview supposed to test?

The written examination is designed to test the technical knowledge and competence of the candidate; the oral is designed to evaluate intangible qualities, not readily measured otherwise, and to establish a list showing the relative fitness of each candidate – as measured against his competitors – for the position sought. Scoring is not on the basis of "right" and "wrong," but on a sliding scale of values ranging from "not passable" to "outstanding." As a matter of fact, it is possible to achieve a relatively low score without a single "incorrect" answer because of evident weakness in the qualities being measured.

Occasionally, an examination may consist entirely of an oral test – either an individual or a group oral. In such cases, information is sought concerning the technical knowledges and abilities of the candidate, since there has been no written examination for this purpose. More commonly, however, an oral test is used to supplement a written examination.

Who conducts interviews?

The composition of oral boards varies among different jurisdictions. In nearly all, a representative of the personnel department serves as chairman. One of the members of the board may be a representative of the department in which the candidate would work. In some cases, "outside experts" are used, and, frequently, a businessman or some other representative of the general public is asked to serve. Labor and management or other special groups may be represented. The aim is to secure the services of experts in the appropriate field.

However the board is composed, it is a good idea (and not at all improper or unethical) to ascertain in advance of the interview who the members are and what groups they represent. When you are introduced to them, you will have some idea of their backgrounds and interests, and at least you will not stutter and stammer over their names.

What should be done before the interview?

While knowledge about the board members is useful and takes some of the surprise element out of the interview, there is other preparation which is more substantive. It *is* possible to prepare for an oral interview – in several ways:

1) Keep a copy of your application and review it carefully before the interview

This may be the only document before the oral board, and the starting point of the interview. Know what education and experience you have listed there, and the sequence and dates of all of it. Sometimes the board will ask you to review the highlights of your experience for them; you should not have to hem and haw doing it.

2) Study the class specification and the examination announcement

Usually, the oral board has one or both of these to guide them. The qualities, characteristics or knowledges required by the position sought are stated in these documents. They offer valuable clues as to the nature of the oral interview. For example, if the job involves supervisory responsibilities, the announcement will usually indicate that knowledge of modern supervisory methods and the qualifications of the candidate as a supervisor will be tested. If so, you can expect such questions, frequently in the form of a hypothetical situation which you are expected to solve. NEVER go into an oral without knowledge of the duties and responsibilities of the job you seek.

3) Think through each qualification required

Try to visualize the kind of questions you would ask if you were a board member. How well could you answer them? Try especially to appraise your own knowledge and background in each area, *measured against the job sought*, and identify any areas in which you are weak. Be critical and realistic – do not flatter yourself.

4) Do some general reading in areas in which you feel you may be weak
   For example, if the job involves supervision and your past experience has NOT, some general reading in supervisory methods and practices, particularly in the field of human relations, might be useful. Do NOT study agency procedures or detailed manuals. The oral board will be testing your understanding and capacity, not your memory.

5) Get a good night's sleep and watch your general health and mental attitude
   You will want a clear head at the interview. Take care of a cold or any other minor ailment, and of course, no hangovers.

What should be done on the day of the interview?
   Now comes the day of the interview itself. Give yourself plenty of time to get there. Plan to arrive somewhat ahead of the scheduled time, particularly if your appointment is in the fore part of the day. If a previous candidate fails to appear, the board might be ready for you a bit early. By early afternoon an oral board is almost invariably behind schedule if there are many candidates, and you may have to wait. Take along a book or magazine to read, or your application to review, but leave any extraneous material in the waiting room when you go in for your interview. In any event, relax and compose yourself.
   The matter of dress is important. The board is forming impressions about you – from your experience, your manners, your attitude, and your appearance. Give your personal appearance careful attention. Dress your best, but not your flashiest. Choose conservative, appropriate clothing, and be sure it is immaculate. This is a business interview, and your appearance should indicate that you regard it as such. Besides, being well groomed and properly dressed will help boost your confidence.
   Sooner or later, someone will call your name and escort you into the interview room. *This is it.* From here on you are on your own. It is too late for any more preparation. But remember, you asked for this opportunity to prove your fitness, and you are here because your request was granted.

What happens when you go in?
   The usual sequence of events will be as follows: The clerk (who is often the board stenographer) will introduce you to the chairman of the oral board, who will introduce you to the other members of the board. Acknowledge the introductions before you sit down. Do not be surprised if you find a microphone facing you or a stenotypist sitting by. Oral interviews are usually recorded in the event of an appeal or other review.
   Usually the chairman of the board will open the interview by reviewing the highlights of your education and work experience from your application – primarily for the benefit of the other members of the board, as well as to get the material into the record. Do not interrupt or comment unless there is an error or significant misinterpretation; if that is the case, do not hesitate. But do not quibble about insignificant matters. Also, he will usually ask you some question about your education, experience or your present job – partly to get you to start talking and to establish the interviewing "rapport." He may start the actual questioning, or turn it over to one of the other members. Frequently, each member undertakes the questioning on a particular area, one in which he is perhaps most competent, so you can expect each member to participate in the examination. Because time is limited, you may also expect some rather abrupt switches in the direction the questioning takes, so do not be upset by it. Normally, a board

member will not pursue a single line of questioning unless he discovers a particular strength or weakness.

After each member has participated, the chairman will usually ask whether any member has any further questions, then will ask you if you have anything you wish to add. Unless you are expecting this question, it may floor you. Worse, it may start you off on an extended, extemporaneous speech. The board is not usually seeking more information. The question is principally to offer you a last opportunity to present further qualifications or to indicate that you have nothing to add. So, if you feel that a significant qualification or characteristic has been overlooked, it is proper to point it out in a sentence or so. Do not compliment the board on the thoroughness of their examination – they have been sketchy, and you know it. If you wish, merely say, "No thank you, I have nothing further to add." This is a point where you can "talk yourself out" of a good impression or fail to present an important bit of information. Remember, *you close the interview yourself.*

The chairman will then say, "That is all, Mr. _____, thank you." Do not be startled; the interview is over, and quicker than you think. Thank him, gather your belongings and take your leave. Save your sigh of relief for the other side of the door.

How to put your best foot forward

Throughout this entire process, you may feel that the board individually and collectively is trying to pierce your defenses, seek out your hidden weaknesses and embarrass and confuse you. Actually, this is not true. They are obliged to make an appraisal of your qualifications for the job you are seeking, and they want to see you in your best light. Remember, they must interview all candidates and a non-cooperative candidate may become a failure in spite of their best efforts to bring out his qualifications. Here are 15 suggestions that will help you:

1) Be natural – Keep your attitude confident, not cocky

If you are not confident that you can do the job, do not expect the board to be. Do not apologize for your weaknesses, try to bring out your strong points. The board is interested in a positive, not negative, presentation. Cockiness will antagonize any board member and make him wonder if you are covering up a weakness by a false show of strength.

2) Get comfortable, but don't lounge or sprawl

Sit erectly but not stiffly. A careless posture may lead the board to conclude that you are careless in other things, or at least that you are not impressed by the importance of the occasion. Either conclusion is natural, even if incorrect. Do not fuss with your clothing, a pencil or an ashtray. Your hands may occasionally be useful to emphasize a point; do not let them become a point of distraction.

3) Do not wisecrack or make small talk

This is a serious situation, and your attitude should show that you consider it as such. Further, the time of the board is limited – they do not want to waste it, and neither should you.

4) Do not exaggerate your experience or abilities

In the first place, from information in the application or other interviews and sources, the board may know more about you than you think. Secondly, you probably will not get away with it. An experienced board is rather adept at spotting such a situation, so do not take the chance.

5) If you know a board member, do not make a point of it, yet do not hide it
   Certainly you are not fooling him, and probably not the other members of the board. Do not try to take advantage of your acquaintanceship – it will probably do you little good.

6) Do not dominate the interview
   Let the board do that. They will give you the clues – do not assume that you have to do all the talking. Realize that the board has a number of questions to ask you, and do not try to take up all the interview time by showing off your extensive knowledge of the answer to the first one.

7) Be attentive
   You only have 20 minutes or so, and you should keep your attention at its sharpest throughout. When a member is addressing a problem or question to you, give him your undivided attention. Address your reply principally to him, but do not exclude the other board members.

8) Do not interrupt
   A board member may be stating a problem for you to analyze. He will ask you a question when the time comes. Let him state the problem, and wait for the question.

9) Make sure you understand the question
   Do not try to answer until you are sure what the question is. If it is not clear, restate it in your own words or ask the board member to clarify it for you. However, do not haggle about minor elements.

10) Reply promptly but not hastily
   A common entry on oral board rating sheets is "candidate responded readily," or "candidate hesitated in replies." Respond as promptly and quickly as you can, but do not jump to a hasty, ill-considered answer.

11) Do not be peremptory in your answers
   A brief answer is proper – but do not fire your answer back. That is a losing game from your point of view. The board member can probably ask questions much faster than you can answer them.

12) Do not try to create the answer you think the board member wants
   He is interested in what kind of mind you have and how it works – not in playing games. Furthermore, he can usually spot this practice and will actually grade you down on it.

13) Do not switch sides in your reply merely to agree with a board member
   Frequently, a member will take a contrary position merely to draw you out and to see if you are willing and able to defend your point of view. Do not start a debate, yet do not surrender a good position. If a position is worth taking, it is worth defending.

14) Do not be afraid to admit an error in judgment if you are shown to be wrong

The board knows that you are forced to reply without any opportunity for careful consideration. Your answer may be demonstrably wrong. If so, admit it and get on with the interview.

15) Do not dwell at length on your present job

The opening question may relate to your present assignment. Answer the question but do not go into an extended discussion. You are being examined for a *new* job, not your present one. As a matter of fact, try to phrase ALL your answers in terms of the job for which you are being examined.

Basis of Rating

Probably you will forget most of these "do's" and "don'ts" when you walk into the oral interview room. Even remembering them all will not ensure you a passing grade. Perhaps you did not have the qualifications in the first place. But remembering them will help you to put your best foot forward, without treading on the toes of the board members.

Rumor and popular opinion to the contrary notwithstanding, an oral board wants you to make the best appearance possible. They know you are under pressure – but they also want to see how you respond to it as a guide to what your reaction would be under the pressures of the job you seek. They will be influenced by the degree of poise you display, the personal traits you show and the manner in which you respond.

ABOUT THIS BOOK

This book contains tests divided into Examination Sections. Go through each test, answering every question in the margin. At the end of each test look at the answer key and check your answers. On the ones you got wrong, look at the right answer choice and learn. Do not fill in the answers first. Do not memorize the questions and answers, but understand the answer and principles involved. On your test, the questions will likely be different from the samples. Questions are changed and new ones added. If you understand these past questions you should have success with any changes that arise. Tests may consist of several types of questions. We have additional books on each subject should more study be advisable or necessary for you. Finally, the more you study, the better prepared you will be. This book is intended to be the last thing you study before you walk into the examination room. Prior study of relevant texts is also recommended. NLC publishes some of these in our Fundamental Series. Knowledge and good sense are important factors in passing your exam. Good luck also helps. So now study this Passbook, absorb the material contained within and take that knowledge into the examination. Then do your best to pass that exam.

EXAMINATION SECTION

EXAMINATION SECTION
TEST 1

DIRECTIONS: Each question or incomplete statement is followed by several suggested answers or completions. Select the one that BEST answers the question or completes the statement. *PRINT THE LETTER OF THE CORRECT ANSWER IN THE SPACE AT THE RIGHT.*

1. The speed disparity between adjacent devices can cause problems with an interface. These problems are usually resolved by temporarily storing input in a(n)

    A. channel
    B. control unit
    C. register
    D. buffer

2. A typical computer spends most of its time

    A. compiling
    B. waiting for input or output
    C. executing instructions
    D. interpreting commands

3. What is the basic input device on a small computer?

    A. Keyboard   B. Cursor   C. Mouse   D. Processor

4. When two hardware devices want to communicate, they will FIRST exchange _____ signals.

    A. interrupt   B. protocol   C. interface   D. boot

5. Which of the following is retrieved and executed by the processor?

    A. Instructions
    B. Clock pulses
    C. Information
    D. Data

6. What type of architecture is used by most microcomputers?

    A. Standard
    B. Serial
    C. Single-bus
    D. Multiple-bus

7. Typically, _____ is NOT a problem associated with a computer's main memory.

    A. cost
    B. volatility
    C. capacity
    D. speed

8. Which of the following types of memory management is the SIMPLEST?

    A. Sector-oriented
    B. Dynamic
    C. Block-oriented
    D. Fixed partition

9. What is the term for the time during which a disk drive is brought up to operating speed and the access device is positioned?

    A. E-time
    B. Rotational delay
    C. Seek time
    D. Access time

1

10. What type of code is written by programmers?

   A. Load module
   B. Source
   C. Object
   D. Operating

11. A _____ is the basic output device on a small computer.

   A. printer
   B. keyboard
   C. display screen
   D. hard disk

12. Which of the following serves to manage a computer's resources?

   A. User
   B. Operating system
   C. Programmer
   D. Software

13. A computer processes data into

   A. information
   B. pulses
   C. code
   D. facts

14. What is the term for the entity used to link external devices to a small computer system?

   A. Interface
   B. Network
   C. Plug-in
   D. Modem

15. For a transaction processing application, a _____ file organization should be selected.

   A. sequential
   B. indexed
   C. direct
   D. random

16. Which element of a microcomputer directly controls input and output?

   A. Buffer
   B. Processor
   C. Bus
   D. Control unit

17. A computer's data and program instructions are stored in

   A. memory
   B. the video buffer
   C. a program
   D. an output port

18. What is the term for the metal framework around which most microcomputers are constructed?

   A. Mainframe
   B. Hard disk
   C. Motherboard
   D. Expansion slot

19. The read/write head of a computer's disk drive is contained on the

   A. magnetic drum
   B. data element
   C. token
   D. access mechanism

20. A(n) _____ is used to link a small computer's secondary storage device to the system.

   A. control unit
   B. interface board
   C. register
   D. buffer

21. What processor management technique is used on most timesharing network systems?

   A. Time-slicing
   B. Command sorting
   C. Apportionment
   D. Interrupt processing

22. Which of the following procedures is used to copy data from a slow-speed device to a high-speed device for eventual input to a program?

    A. Queuing
    B. Spooling
    C. Buffing
    D. Scheduling

23. A location in memory is located by its

    A. section   B. register   C. address   D. decoder

24. _____ data is represented by a wave.

    A. Microwave   B. Digital   C. Binary   D. Analog

25. A programmer defines the logical structure of a problem by using a(n)

    A. assembler
    B. compiler
    C. interpreter
    D. nonprocedural language

KEY (CORRECT ANSWERS)

1. D
2. B
3. A
4. B
5. A

6. C
7. D
8. D
9. C
10. B

11. C
12. B
13. A
14. A
15. C

16. B
17. A
18. C
19. D
20. B

21. A
22. B
23. C
24. D
25. D

TEST 2

DIRECTIONS: Each question or incomplete statement is followed by several suggested answers or completions. Select the one that BEST answers the question or completes the statement. *PRINT THE LETTER OF THE CORRECT ANSWER IN THE SPACE AT THE RIGHT.*

1. Data is converted from digital to analog form through the process of
   - A. demodulation
   - B. teleporting
   - C. cross-modulation
   - D. modulation

2. Which of the following represents the simplest data structure?
   - A. Record
   - B. File
   - C. List
   - D. Directory

3. The term for a set of parallel wires used to transmit data, commands, or power is
   - A. bus
   - B. cabling
   - C. line
   - D. twisted pair

4. _____ limit the number of peripherals that can be linked to a microcomputer system.
   - A. Channels
   - B. Bus lines
   - C. Buffers
   - D. Slots

5. A data structure in which memory is allocated as a series of numbered cells is a(n)
   - A. array
   - B. block
   - C. record
   - D. register

6. On a disk, each program's name and location can be located on the
   - A. index
   - B. address
   - C. label
   - D. register

7. Onto which of the following structures is a processing chip stored?
   - A. Board
   - B. Plate
   - C. Bus
   - D. Disk

8. Two or more independent processors can share the same memory under a system known as
   - A. time-sharing
   - B. FAT binaries
   - C. multitasking
   - D. multiprocessing

9. A _____ is the basic storage unit around which a microcomputer system is designed.
   - A. bit
   - B. block
   - C. word
   - D. byte

10. A user communicates with an operating system by means of a(n)
    - A. interface
    - B. peripheral
    - C. command language
    - D. application

11. A _____ is used to convert data from pulse form to wave form and back again.
    - A. channel
    - B. modem
    - C. SCSI port
    - D. bus

12. Data values can be accessed according to their element numbers in a(n)
    - A. list
    - B. register
    - C. record
    - D. array

13. Under a _____ memory management scheme, a program is allocated as much memory as it needs.

    A. sector-oriented
    B. dynamic
    C. block-oriented
    D. fixed partition

14. What is the term for the process of removing errors from a program?

    A. Compiling
    B. Debugging
    C. Troubleshooting
    D. Extraction

15. _____ is the term for the time during which a desired sector of a disk approaches the access device.

    A. Run time
    B. Rotational delay
    C. Seek time
    D. Access time

16. What is the term for the process by which a networked computer selects the terminal it will communicate with?

    A. Compiling
    B. Polling
    C. Interfacing
    D. Selection

17. After compilers and assemblers read a programmer's code, they generate a(n)

    A. object module
    B. nonprocedural language
    C. subroutine
    D. load module

18. Memory that loses its content when the machine's power is turned off is described as

    A. read-only
    B. redundant
    C. dependent
    D. volatile

19. Which module of an operating system sends primitive commands to a disk drive?

    A. Motherboard
    B. IOCS
    C. CPU
    D. Command processor

20. The BASIC measure of data communications speed is

    A. bit rate
    B. baud rate
    C. kilobytes per second
    D. bits per second

21. The term _____ is used to denote a single, meaningful data element, such as a person's telephone number.

    A. field
    B. item
    C. record
    D. file

22. What is the term for the machine-level translation of a programmer's source code?

    A. Load module
    B. Subroutine
    C. Source library
    D. Object module

23. Which part of an instruction directs the actions of the processor?

    A. Pulse
    B. Operation code
    C. Statement
    D. Operand

24. A _____ is used to store programs that enter a multiprogramming system.

    A. tape
    B. spool
    C. buffer
    D. queue

25. _____ is a device used to avoid data dependency and redundancy.

    A. Sequential filing   B. Continuous backup
    C. Random filing   D. Database

KEY (CORRECT ANSWERS)

1.	A		11.	B
2.	C		12.	D
3.	A		13.	B
4.	D		14.	B
5.	A		15.	B
6.	A		16.	B
7.	A		17.	A
8.	D		18.	D
9.	C		19.	B
10.	C		20.	B

21. A
22. D
23. B
24. D
25. D

EXAMINATION SECTION
TEST 1

DIRECTIONS: Each question or incomplete statement is followed by several suggested answers or completions. Select the one that BEST answers the question or completes the statement. *PRINT THE LETTER OF THE CORRECT ANSWER IN THE SPACE AT THE RIGHT.*

1. In considering a new word processing system for a regional office, which of the following would MOST likely be the MOST important consideration in making a decision?

    A. Ease of operation
    B. Friendliness of service technicians
    C. Availability of service technicians
    D. Capacity of the system to meet the unit's word processing needs

    1.____

2. Your supervisor is out of town for several days and has asked you to act as supervisor in his absence. An employee in the unit comes to you and complains that the supervisor has been dividing the workload unfairly.
Of the following, the MOST appropriate action for you to take is

    A. defend the actions of your supervisor
    B. encourage the employee to file a grievance
    C. listen to the employee attentively
    D. explain to the employee that you have no authority to handle the situation

    2.____

3. A principal stenographer still on probation is instructed to supervise and coordinate the completion of a large word processing project. Her supervisor asks her how long she thinks the project will take. The principal stenographer gives her supervisor an estimate that is two days longer than she actually thinks the project will take to complete. The project is completed two days earlier, and the principal stenographer is congratulated by her supervisor for her efforts.
In purposely overestimating the time required to complete the project, the principal stenographer showed

    A. *good* judgment because it helped her appear very efficient
    B. *good* judgment because it helps keep unrealistic supervisors from expecting too much
    C. *poor* judgment because plans and schedules of other components of the project may have been based on her false estimate
    D. *poor* judgment because she should have used the extra time to further check and, proofread the work

    3.____

4. Which of the following would MOST likely be the MOST important in providing support to one's supervisor?

    A. Screening annoying phone calls
    B. Reviewing and forwarding articles and publications that may be of interest to your supervisor
    C. Correctly transmitting instructions from the supervisor to appropriate staff members
    D. Reviewing outgoing correspondence for proper grammatical usage and clarity

    4.____

2 (#1)

5. While you are on the telephone answering a question about your agency, a visitor comes to your desk and starts to ask you a question. There is no emergency or urgency in either situation, that of the phone call or that of answering the visitor's question.
In this case, you should

   A. excuse yourself to the person on the telephone and tell the visitor that you will be with him or her as soon as you have finished on the phone
   B. explain to the person on the phone that you have a visitor and must shorten the conversation
   C. continue to talk with the person on the phone while looking up occasionally at the visitor to let him or her know that you know he or she is there
   D. continue to talk with the person on the telephone until you are finished and then let the visitor know that you're sorry to have kept him or her waiting

6. Your supervisor is out of town on vacation for one week, and asks you to act as supervisor in her absence. The second day she is gone a very important, complex budgetary form, which must be responded to in ten days, arrives in your unit.
Of the following, it would be BEST if you

   A. filled out the form and submitted it as soon as possible
   B. read the form over, did any time-consuming research that might be needed, and then gave the uncompleted form to your supervisor as soon as she returned
   C. asked for help from your supervisor's supervisor in completing the form
   D. tried to contact your supervisor for advice

7. Of the following, which would MOST likely be of the highest priority?
The typing of

   A. a grant proposal due next week
   B. new addresses onto a mailing list for a future mailing
   C. a payroll form for a new employee that needs to be submitted immediately
   D. a memorandum from the Commissioner to all employees regarding new procedures

8. Your office is moving to a new location.
Of the following, it would be MOST important to ensure that

   A. others will know your office's new address and phone number
   B. the new office space is comfortable
   C. your supervisor is happy with his or her new office space
   D. the move itself goes smoothly

9. Of the following, which would generally be considered the LEAST desirable?

   A. Accidentally disconnecting an executive from an important phone call
   B. Ordering the wrong back-up part for a copying machine
   C. Misplacing several hundred dollars worth of personal checks payable to your department
   D. Misplacing a memorandum that needs to be typed

10. Your supervisor has told you not to let anyone disturb her for the rest of the morning unless absolutely necessary because she has some urgent work to complete. The department head telephones and asks to speak to her.
The BEST course of action for you to take is to

    A. ask the department head if he or she can leave a message
    B. ask your supervisor if she can take the call
    C. tell the department head that your supervisor is out
    D. let your supervisor know that her instructions have put you in a difficult position

10.____

11. Which of the following would be MOST likely to contribute to efficiency in the operation of an office?

    A. A new computer system is instituted in an office.
    B. The employees are paid well.
    C. Procedures and practices are studied for any redundant operations.
    D. A supervisor delegates work.

11.____

12. You are at work at your desk on a special project when a visitor approaches you. You cannot interrupt your work to take care of this person.
Of the following, the BEST and MOST courteous way of handling this situation is to

    A. avoid looking up from your work until you are finished with what you are doing
    B. tell the visitor that you will not be able to assist him or her for quite some time
    C. refer the individual to another employee who can take care of him or her right away
    D. chat with the individual while you continue to work

12.____

13. Which of the following would MOST likely be of the highest priority?
A(n)

    A. annual report due next month
    B. irate member of the public who is standing at your desk
    C. important financial report requested by the Commissioner
    D. memorandum to all employees outlining very important new policy needs to be typed and distributed immediately

13.____

14. Someone uses *special pull* to obtain the services of your unit at the last minute. You and the four employees you supervise have done everything you could do to provide good service, and you feel things have gone very well. The client is not pleased, however, and enters your office and begins screaming at you and the other employees present.
Of the following, it would be BEST if you

    A. ignored the person
    B. tried to calm the person down
    C. asked the person to leave the office
    D. called your supervisor in to help handle the situation

14.____

15. Your supervisor is on vacation for two weeks, and you have been asked to fill in for her. Your office is very busy, and there is a strict procedure for filling requests. Leslie from Unit X wants something completed immediately. You don't feel this is possible or reasonable, and politely explain why to Leslie. Leslie becomes very angry and says that she will complain to your supervisor about your uncooperative behavior as soon as your supervisor returns.
Of the following, it would be BEST if you

   A. filled Leslie's request
   B. reported Leslie to her supervisor
   C. complained to your supervisor about the situation as soon as she returned
   D. stood by your decision once you determined it was correct

KEY (CORRECT ANSWERS)

1. D	6. B	11. C
2. C	7. C	12. C
3. C	8. A	13. B
4. C	9. C	14. B
5. A	10. B	15. D

EXAMINATION SECTION

TEST 1

DIRECTIONS: Each question or incomplete statement is followed by several suggested answers or completions. Select the one that BEST answers the question or completes the statement. *PRINT THE LETTER OF THE CORRECT ANSWER IN THE SPACE AT THE RIGHT.*

1. Which of the following must be changed in order to implement a word processing system?
    A. Equipment
    B. Procedures
    C. Work relationships between people
    D. Methods of supervision
    E. All of the above

2. A type of word processing hardware/software configuration where several terminals share the same CPU is called a _____ configuration.
    A. shared logic
    B. single-user
    C. distributed logic
    D. multifunction
    E. timesharing

3. Current technology has led word processing hardware/software configurations toward
    A. centralized processing
    B. decentralized processing
    C. the use of mainframe computers
    D. the use of wide-area networks
    E. the increasing use of minicomputers over microcomputers to do word processing

4. A(n) _____ printer offers *letter quality* print.
    A. daisy wheel
    B. dot matrix
    C. laser
    D. ink jet
    E. all of the above

5. A _____ is an input device or software that can read handwritten or printed data, which may be later edited by a word processor.
    A. MICR
    B. OCR
    C. laser reader
    D. daisy wheel
    E. both A and B

6. A(n) _____ uses special software to do word processing functions.   6._____
   A. word processor   B. electronic typewriter
   C. computer processor   D. automatic typewriter
   E. electronic printer

7. Printed output is called   7._____
   A. soft copy   B. printout
   C. formatted output   D. hard copy
   E. none of the above

8. _____ transmits a word-processed document via electronic   8._____
   communications.
   A. TWX   B. Telecopy
   C. E-mail   D. Telex
   E. Modem

9. _____ refers to output on a video screen or computer monitor.   9._____
   A. Soft copy   B. Video copy
   C. Light output   D. Hard copy
   E. None of the above

10. _____ refers to output to microfilm instead of paper or video.   10._____
    A. TWX   B. Microfiche
    C. COM   D. Floppy disk output
    E. None of the above

11. A disadvantage of word processors is   11._____
    A. decreased effective typing speeds
    B. higher costs in producing documents
    C. that offices with word processors generate more paper than
       offices without word processors
    D. lower quality output than computer printers
    E. difficult revision of previously processed documents

12. Which of the following is a character that can be entered through a word   12._____
    processor?
    A. %   B. !
    C. [blank space]   D. +
    E. All of the above

13. A _____ can permanently store documents and files.   13._____
    A. printer   B. compact disc
    C. computer memory   D. CPU
    E. All of the above

14. Printers, disk drives, video screens and keyboards are examples of _____ equipment.
    A. output
    B. input
    C. processing
    D. peripheral
    E. storage

15. A _____ features multi-color display.
    A. monochrome monitor
    B. plotter
    C. color monitor
    D. RGB output
    E. graphics monitor

16. A(n) _____ printer forms characters by using a printhead to press pinpoints against a ribbon.
    A. laser
    B. ink jet
    C. daisy wheel
    D. dot matrix
    E. All of the above

17. Which of the following is NOT an input device that may be used on a word processor?
    A. Mouse
    B. Keyboard
    C. Document scanner
    D. DVD
    E. All of the above

18. The _____ is the position on the word processor screen that indicates where the next character will appear.
    A. pointer
    B. cell indicator
    C. status line
    D. cursor
    E. video pointer

19. Which of the following functions allows the upward and downward movement of text lines on the screen?
    A. Cursor keys
    B. Scrolling
    C. Positioning
    D. Page breaking
    E. Blocking

20. Which of the following functions allows text to be indicated for operations such as moving or copying?
    A. Cursor keys
    B. Scrolling
    C. Boilerplating
    D. Page breaking
    E. Blocking

21. Which of the following types of word processing allows the operator to see on the screen *exactly* how the output will appear on paper?
    A. Text-formatted word processing
    B. WYSIWYG
    C. Off-screen formatting
    D. Typeset word processing
    E. Desktop publishing

21._____

22. Most word processors work with a screen length of _____ characters.
    A. 24
    B. 50
    C. 65
    D. 80
    E. None of the above

22._____

23. Most word processor screens will display _____ lines of text at a time.
    A. 80
    B. 50
    C. 32
    D. 24
    E. None of the above

23._____

24. Which of the following features is used to display information about a document being edited on the word processor, including the name of the document, line number and column number?
    A. ruler line
    B. carriage bar
    C. status line
    D. insert line
    E. tab set line

24._____

25. The _____ is used on the word processor screen to resemble the column and margin settings on a typewriter.
    A. ruler line
    B. carriage bar
    C. status line
    D. insert line
    E. tab set line

25._____

KEY (CORRECT ANSWERS)

1. E	11. C	21. B
2. A	12. E	22. D
3. B	13. B	23. D
4. E	14. D	24. C
5. B	15. C	25. A
6. A	16. D	
7. D	17. D	
8. C	18. D	
9. A	19. B	
10. C	20. E	

TEST 2

DIRECTIONS: Each question or incomplete statement is followed by several suggested answers or completions. Select the one that BEST answers the question or completes the statement. *PRINT THE LETTER OF THE CORRECT ANSWER IN THE SPACE AT THE RIGHT.*

1. Which of the following word-processing features enables the programmer to type characters continuously without pressing the carriage return at the end of the line?
    A. Insert
    B. Wraparound
    C. Continuous type
    D. Boilerplating
    E. Reformatting

    1._____

2. A _____ carriage return is placed into a document by the word processor, not by the operator.
    A. hard
    B. soft
    C. embedded
    D. non-embedded
    E. none of the above

    2._____

3. The spacing of words and letters within a line of type to make it meet both margins of a column is called
    A. boilerplating
    B. justification
    C. margin alignment
    D. microjustification
    E. proportional spacing

    3._____

4. The spacing between characters and words on a line can be more evenly separated with
    A. justification
    B. boilerplating
    C. microjustification
    D. margin alignment
    E. all of the above

    4._____

5. Commands placed into a document which affect the placement, shape and size of margins, headings, footings, and page numbers are called _____ commands.
    A. on-screen format
    B. embedded format
    C. boilerplate embedded
    D. dot
    E. all of the above

    5._____

6. On a standard sheet of 11" x 8.5" paper, how many vertical lines are available for printing?
    A. 6
    B. 11
    C. 50
    D. 66
    E. none of the above

    6._____

7. The study of the interaction between humans and machines is called
   A. ornithology
   B. metaphysics
   C. robotics
   D. ergonomics
   E. mechahumanism

8. When the _____ key is held down, the character will be entered continuously until the key is released.
   A. alphabetic
   B. Dvorak
   C. numeric
   D. Qwerty
   E. auto-repeat

9. This is a *toggle* key. When you press it, all alphabetic characters will be in uppercase. When you press it again, all alphabetic characters will be lowercase. This is the _____ key.
   A. numeric
   B. page down
   C. Alt
   D. caps lock
   E. return

10. On most word-processing machines, the _____ keys execute a special function such as saving a document or centering a line of text.
    A. Esc
    B. Ctrl
    C. function
    D. Alt
    E. All of the above

11. A _____ is an input device which can read data from printed or typed documents and enter it into the computer for further editing.
    A. scanner
    B. modem
    C. tracer
    D. TWX
    E. fax

12. A printing term for fully formed characters is
    A. draft quality
    B. double strike
    C. letter quality
    D. dot matrix
    E. near letter quality

13. _____ paper is used for printed output. It consists of individual sheets connected together, and perforated for easy detachment.
    A. single sheet
    B. fanfold
    C. continuous form
    D. Both A and B
    E. Both B and C

14. The particular style and size in which a character may be printed is called
    A. typestyle
    B. font
    C. display
    D. pixel
    E. density

15. Which of the following is an external storage media on which documents may be stored and retrieved from?
    A. Floppy disk
    B. Hard disk
    C. Compact disc
    D. External hard drive
    E. All of the above

15._____

16. Before a new floppy disk may be used on a specific word processor, it must be prepared for use with the word processor through a process called
    A. initializing
    B. formatting
    C. booting
    D. consolidation
    E. both B and C

16._____

17. A 10-megabyte hard disk can store the equivalent of _____ 360K floppy disks.
    A. 21
    B. 23
    C. 25
    D. 27
    E. 29

17._____

18. Generally speaking, how often should documents stored on computer disks be backed up for security and safety reasons?
    A. Annually
    B. Monthly
    C. Weekly
    D. Daily
    E. Multiple times daily

18._____

19. A method of document distribution in which a printed copy of the document may be sent over telephone lines is
    A. modemizing
    B. e-mail
    C. fax transmission
    D. digital transmission
    E. analog transmission

19._____

20. The _____ communicates between the word-processing hardware and software.
    A. operating system
    B. database system
    C. applications program
    D. command processor
    E. input/output manager

20._____

21. A listing of documents or files stored on a particular disk is called a
    A. catalog
    B. inventory
    C. directory
    D. data storage program
    E. menu

21._____

22. To facilitate the organization of documents on the disk, the _____ directory may be subdivided into other classifications of directories.
    A. root
    B. main
    D. sub
    D. path
    E. core

22._____

4 (#2)

23. A _____ word-processing software help system displays help messages based upon the command being used at the moment.
    A. menu-driven
    B. context-sensitive
    C. command-driven
    D. reference-sensitive
    E. key-sensitive

23._____

24. A _____ word processor allows the user to choose an operation to be performed from a list of options.
    A. command-driven
    B. context-sensitive
    C. reference-sensitive
    D. menu-driven
    E. icon-driven

24._____

25. The _____ menu is usually used with a mouse. The menu descends from the top of the screen after it is pointed to by the mouse.
    A. pop-up
    B. sticky
    C. pull-down
    D. multi-level
    D. menu tree

25._____

KEY (CORRECT ANSWERS)

1. B	11. A	21. C
2. B	12. C	22. A
3. B	13. C	23. B
4. C	14. B	24. D
5. B	15. E	25. C
6. D	16. B	
7. D	17. D	
8. E	18. D	
9. D	19. C	
10. C	20. A	

EXAMINATION SECTION
TEST 1

DIRECTIONS: Each question or incomplete statement is followed by several suggested answers or completions. Select the one that BEST answers the question or completes the statement. *PRINT THE LETTER OF THE CORRECT ANSWER IN THE SPACE AT THE RIGHT.*

1. When a document has been previously saved on a disk, and the command is issued to save the document again, the

    A. document is erased from the disk
    B. document is stored in two different forms on the disk
    C. latest version of the document is saved and replaces the previous version
    D. document will not be saved
    E. document is erased from both the screen and disk

    1.____

2. If a previously saved document is being edited and the word processing operator does not want to save the new changes, the operator should

    A. turn off the machine
    B. save the document
    C. abandon the document without saving it
    D. rename the document
    E. reverse all previous editing changes one by one

    2.____

3. In a word-processed document, a period at the end of a sentence should be followed by_____ space(s).

    A. zero   B. one
    C. two   D. three
    E. one, two or three

    3.____

4. When a text is entered the_____ acts as a *signal* that the word processor automatically enters while wrapping words to the next line

    A. hard carriage return   B. soft carriage return
    C. hard space   D. soft space
    E. both A and C

    4.____

5. With_____ the word processing operator may move a document up and down, line by line on the screen.

    A. horizontal scrolling   B. vertical scrolling
    C. paging   D. diagonal scrolling
    E. none of the above

    5.____

6. On the word processor, the_____ mode overwrites any previously typed text.

    A. insert   B. overwrite
    C. strikeover   D. delete
    E. all of the above

    6.____

7. Two hyphenated words connected by the _____ will not split at the right margin and will always appear on the same line.

   A. soft hyphen
   B. hard hyphen
   C. soft carriage return
   D. hard carriage return
   E. hard space

8. The realignment of text after editing so that it is aligned with the margins is called

   A. paragraph reform
   B. pagination
   C. repagination
   D. blocking
   E. re-editing

9. A function used to calculate or recalculate page breaks on a document is called

   A. repagination
   B. paragraph reform
   C. document reform
   D. blocking
   E. paging

10. The process of moving and copying a block of text from one place to another is called

    A. blocking
    B. moving
    C. copying
    D. cutting and pasting
    E. all of the above

11. A string of characters may consist of which kinds of characters?

    A. Numbers
    B. Letters
    C. Special characters (*,!,&, etc.)
    D. Phrases
    E. All of the above

12. A *search and replace* option which finds all occurrences of a search item and automatically replaces it is called _____ search and replace.

    A. item
    B. case-sensitive
    C. automatic
    D. wildcard
    E. global

13. Assume you wish to search for the word "row." You specify that the search NOT be case sensitive. In which of the following phrases would the word be found?

    A. Rowboat
    B. Front Row Seats
    C. Arrow
    D. Row, row, row your boat
    E. All of the above

14. A program used by the word-processing software to find a synonym for a certain word in a document is a(n)

    A. algorithm
    B. spell checker
    C. style and grammar checker
    D. thesaurus
    E. all of the above

15. The settings initially entered into word processing software by its designers indicate initial settings, such as the right and left margins, or perhaps the number of lines per page. These settings can usually be changed by the user.
    This refers to

    A. default settings
    B. configuration settings
    C. set-up file
    D. initialization settings
    E. format settings

16. A single line ending a paragraph that appears by itself at the top of a page is called a(n)

    A. widow
    B. orphan
    C. single line paragraph
    D. soft page break
    E. hard page break

17. The first line of a paragraph that appears by itself as the last line of a page is called a(n)

    A. widow
    B. orphan
    C. single line paragraph
    D. soft page break
    E. hard page break

18. A specific code in one page of a document refers to a page or other number elsewhere in the document. The code always correctly displays the number to which it refers even if that number is changed.
    This paragraph describes the feature known as

    A. automatic page breaking
    B. hard page breaking
    C. symbolic referencing
    D. repagination
    E. formatting

19. _____ allows entire pages of text to be centered in the middle of the page.

    A. Horizontal alignment
    B. Centering
    C. Vertical alignment
    D. Justification
    E. Blocking

20. _____ refers to the number of characters printed per inch.

    A. Pica
    B. Elite
    C. Microjustification
    D. Helvetica
    E. Pitch

21. Which of the following is NOT a typeface?

    A. Elite
    B. Pica
    C. Times Roman
    D. Helvetica
    E. Hearst

22. Of the following, which is the SMALLEST type size?

    A. 8 pitch
    B. 8 point
    C. 10 point
    D. 10 pitch
    E. 14 point

23. A certain method assigns more or less space to characters based upon their width. For example, the letter "i" is given less space than the letter "m" when printed.
    This refers to

    A. fixed spacing
    B. fixed pitch
    C. proportional spacing
    D. microjustification
    E. justification

24. The _____ comes on a floppy or hard disk. It is loaded into the memory of the word processor, and is used when needed.

    A. internal font
    B. cartridge font
    C. font server
    D. memory font
    E. downloadable font

25. Columns of numbers which may include decimal points are aligned with

    A. justification
    B. horizontal tabs
    C. decimal tabs
    D. tab stops
    E. tab columns

25._____

KEY (CORRECT ANSWERS)

1.	C		11.	E
2.	C		12.	E
3.	C		13.	E
4.	B		14.	D
5.	A		15.	A
6.	C		16.	A
7.	B		17.	B
8.	A		18.	C
9.	A		19.	C
10.	D		20.	E

21. E
22. B
23. C
24. E
25. C

TEST 2

DIRECTIONS: Each question or incomplete statement is followed by several suggested answers or completions. Select the one that BEST answers the question or completes the statement. *PRINT THE LETTER OF THE CORRECT ANSWER IN THE SPACE AT THE RIGHT.*

1. Examine the following paragraph: 1.____
    Working with a word processor allows a person to be more productive than when working with a typewriter.
    This type of indentation is called a(n):

    A. hanging indent B. reverse indent
    C. outdent D. all of the above
    E. none of the above

2. Which of the following contains a superscript? 2.____

    A. Copyright© B. 70°
    C. H$_2$O D. word
    E. none of the above

3. While a document is being printed, the word processing operator may wish to *set up* other documents so that they may begin being printed when a previous document has finished printing. To accomplish this, the operator may use a 3.____

    A. spooler B. print queue
    C. line transmitter D. batch file
    E. delay tray

4. Printing a document along the wide axis of the page, as shown below, is called _____ mode. 4.____

    A. landscape B. portrait
    C. lengthwise D. widthwise
    E. axis

5. When creating a merged document in order to print form letters, the document which contains the unchanging parts of the letter is called the 5.____

    A. variable document B. boilerplate
    C. secondary file D. primary document
    E. all of the above

6. With secondary files to be merged into a file, each individual item that makes up a record in the secondary file is called a 6.____

    A. file B. character
    C. item D. record
    E. database

7. Arranging data in order by last name and code number is called 7.____

    A. arranging B. indexing
    C. sorting D. placement
    E. relative positioning

8. The word processor uses the _____ code to represent special characters, regular characters, and numbers.

   A. binary
   B. hexadecimal
   C. octal
   D. ASCII
   E. OCR

9. The type of columnar output seen in newspaper, newsletter, or magazine output is called

   A. snaking columns
   B. newsletter columns
   C. magazine columns
   D. flowing columns
   E. bulleting

10. _____ is where white characters are printed against a black background.

    A. Kerning
    B. Dropout type
    C. Leading
    D. Reverse video
    E. Inverse video

11. When using a word processor to do desktop publishing, the type of video monitor that is MOST desirable is the

    A. high resolution monochrome
    B. color with VGA
    C. color with EGA
    D. color with UGA
    E. low resolution monochrome

12. A divided or sectioned video screen that allows you to look at two or more parts of the same document or two different documents at once is the

    A. vertical loop
    B. window
    C. submenu
    D. alternate view file
    E. kern

13. A recording of a set of keystrokes repeatedly played over and over again with just the touch of one or a few keystrokes is described as

    A. kerning
    B. leading
    C. macro
    D. program
    E. stored instructions

14. On word processors which can perform arithmetic operations, which key would be used to perform multiplication?

    A. x
    B. X
    C. *
    D. ^
    E. /

15. If performing an arithmetic function with a word processor, the outcome of the following function - (100 + 200 x 5) - would be

    A. 305
    B. 1,500
    C. 500
    D. 1,100
    E. none of the above

16. If a word processor wished to send a document to a remote word processor via telephone lines, the operator would use_____to transmit the document.

    A. TWX
    B. modem
    C. modulator
    D. demodulator
    E. CCD

17. If a *write protect tab* is affixed to the write protect notch on a disk,

    A. both reading and writing can take place on the disk
    B. only reading may take place from the disk
    C. only writing may take place to the disk
    D. neither reading or writing may take place
    E. only previously stored documents may be read from and written to the disk

18. A_____is used in a search, or search and replace option, to represent characters in the same position in the string being searched for

    A. delimiter
    B. wild card
    C. replace character
    D. op character
    E. search string

19. The most important advantage of using a word processor instead of a typewriter is the ability to

    A. print documents at high speed
    B. easily revise and edit documents
    C. store large amounts of data on computer disk
    D. automatically check documents for spelling
    E. print multiple copies of a single document

20. The greatest benefit derived by a company that uses word processing is

    A. cost savings
    B. greater employee productivity and efficiency
    C. better looking documents
    D. a "paperless" office
    E. all of the above

21. _____paper allows for carbonless copies.

    A. Carbon
    B. Continuous form
    C. Impact
    D. Action
    E. Bursting

22. The_____is NOT a word processor peripheral device.

    A. printer
    B. diskdrive
    C. video display
    D. keyboard
    E. memory

23. Documents that are to be bound usually must have a larger margin on the left-hand side to accommodate binding.
This distance is measured by

    A. page offset
    B. left margin offset
    C. left justification
    D. microjustification
    E. binding margin

24. Some word processors allow the documents to be integrated with other computer software packages. One type of computer software package that arranges numbers in columns and rows for arithmetic analysis is called a(n)

    A. database management system
    B. utility program
    C. records management system
    D. calculator program
    E. electronic spreadsheet

25. Assume that the asterisk (*) is a *wild card* character for performing a search function on the word processor. If we wanted to search for the text entitled "National Learning Corporation," or any part thereof, a valid search string would be

    A. National * Corporation
    B. National Learning * Corporation
    C. ******** Learning Corporation
    D. ******** LEARNING CORPORATION
    E. they are all valid

KEY (CORRECT ANSWERS)

1.	D		11.	A
2.	B		12.	B
3.	B		13.	C
4.	A		14.	C
5.	B		15.	D
6.	D		16.	B
7.	C		17.	B
8.	D		18.	B
9.	A		19.	B
10.	B		20.	B

21. D
22. E
23. A
24. E
25. C

EXAMINATION SECTION
TEST 1

DIRECTIONS: Each question or incomplete statement is followed by several suggested answers or completions. Select the one that BEST answers the question or completes the statement. *PRINT THE LETTER OF THE CORRECT ANSWER IN THE SPACE AT THE RIGHT.*

1. The ʌ or caret symbol is a proofreader's mark which means that a
   A. space should have been left between two words
   B. new paragraph should be indicated
   C. word, phrase, or punctuation mark should be inserted
   D. word that is abbreviated should be spelled out

2. Of the following items, the one which should NOT be omitted from a typed inter-office memorandum is the
   A. salutation
   B. complementary closing
   C. formal signature
   D. names of those to receive copies

3. A typed rough draft should be double-spaced and should have wide margins PRIMARILY in order to
   A. save time in making typing corrections
   B. provide room for making insertions and corrections
   C. insure that the report is well-organized
   D. permit faster typing of the draft

4. In tabular reports, when a main heading, secondary heading, and single line of columnar headings are used, a triple space (2 blank lines) would be used after the _____ heading(s).
   A. main
   B. secondary
   C. columnar
   D. main and secondary

5. You have been requested to type a letter to Mr. Brown, a district attorney of a small town.
   Of the following, the CORRECT salutation to use is Dear
   A. District Attorney Brown:
   B. Mr. District Attorney:
   C. Mr. Brown:
   D. Honorable Brown:

6. A form letter that is sent to the public can be made to look more personal in appearance by doing all of the following EXCEPT
   A. using a meter stamp on the envelope of the letter
   B. having the letter signed with pen and ink
   C. using a good quality of paper for the letter
   D. matching the type used in the letter with that used for fill-ins

7. A senior typist opens a word-processing application to instruct a typist to create a table that contains three column headings. Under each column heading are three items.
Of the following, which sequence should the senior typist tell the typist to use when creating this table?
   A. First type the headings, and then type the items under them, a column at a time
   B. type each heading with its column of items under it, one column at a time
   C. first type the column of items, then center the headings above them
   D. type the headings and items across the page line by line

7.____

8. When a letter is addressed to an agency and a particular person should see it, an *attention line* is used.
This attention line is USUALLY found
   A. on the envelope only
   B. above the address
   C. below the address
   D. after the agency named in the address

8.____

9. The typing technique of *justifying* is used to
   A. decide how wide margins of different sized letters should be
   B. make all the lines of copy end evenly on the right-hand margin
   C. center headings above columns on tabular typed material
   D. condense the amount of space that is needed to make a manuscript look presentable

9.____

10. The date line on a letter is typed correctly when the date is ALL on one line
    A. with the month written out   B. with slashes between the numbers
    C. and the month is abbreviated   D. with a period at the end

10.____

11. When considering how wide to make a column when typing a table, the BASIC rule to follow is that the column should be as wide as the longest
    A. item in the body of the column
    B. heading of all of the columns
    C. item in the body or heading of that column
    D. heading or the longest item in the body of any column on that page

11.____

12. When a lengthy quotation is included in a letter or a report, it must be indicated that it is quoted material. This may be done by
    A. enclosing the quotation in parentheses
    B. placing an exclamation point at the end of the quotation
    C. using the apostrophe marks
    D. indenting from the regular margins on the left and right

12.____

13. In order to reach the highest rate of speed and the greatest degree of accuracy while typing, it is LEAST important to
    A. maintain good posture
    B. keep the hands and arms at a comfortable level
    C. strike the keys evenly
    D. keep the typing action in the wrists

14. It has been shown that the rate of typing and dictation drops when the secretary is not familiar with the language or topic of the copy.
    A practice that a supervisor might BEST advise to improve the knowledge and therefore increase the rate of typing dictation for such material would be for the secretary to
    A. plan a conference with her supervisor to discuss the subject matter
    B. read and review correspondence and related technical journals that come into the office
    C. recopy or retype previously transcribed material as practice
    D. withdraw sample materials from the files to take home for study

15. The one of the following in which the tab key is NOT generally used is the
    A. placement of the complimentary close and signature line
    B. indentation of paragraphs
    C. placement of the date line
    D. centering of title headings

16. In order for a business letter to be effective, it is LEAST important that it
    A. say what is meant simply and directly
    B. be written in formal language
    C. include all information the receiver needs to know
    D. be courteously written

17. If you are momentarily called away from your desk while typing a report of a confidential nature, you should cover or turn the copy over and
    A. remove the page being typed from the computer and file the report
    B. ask someone to watch your desk for you
    C. close the document so that the page is not visible
    D. spread a folder over the computer screen to conceal it

18. When typing a table that contains a column of figures and a column of words, the PROPER alignment of the column of figures and the column of words should be an even _____ the column of words.
    A. right-hand edge for the column of numbers and an even left-hand edge for
    B. right-hand edge for both the column of numbers and
    C. left-hand edge for the column of numbers and an even right-hand edge for
    D. left-hand edge for both the column of numbers and

19. The word *re*, when used in a memorandum, refers to the information that is on the _____ line.
    A. identification   B. subject   C. attention   D. reference

19.____

20. Of the following uses of the period, the one which requires NO spacing after it when it is typed is when the period
    A. follows an abbreviation or an initial
    B. follows a figure or letter at the beginning of a line in a list of items
    C. comes between the initials that make up a single abbreviation
    D. comes at the end of a sentence

20.____

21. This mark is a proofreader's mark meaning the word
    A. is misspelled
    B. should be underlined
    C. should be bold
    D. should be capitalized

21.____

22. When typing a report that is double-spaced, the STANDARD recommended practice for indicating the start of new paragraphs is to
    A. double-space between paragraphs and indent the first word at least five spaces
    B. triple-space between paragraphs and indent the first word at least five spaces
    C. triple-space between paragraphs and type block style at the margin
    D. double-space between paragraphs and type block style at the margin

22.____

23. In order to center a heading on a sheet of paper once the center of the paper has been found, the EASIEST and MOST efficient method to use is
    A. note the scale at each end of the heading to be centered and divide by two
    B. backspace from the center of the paper one space for every two letters and spaces in the heading
    C. arrange the heading around the middle number on the computer
    D. use a ruler to mark off the amount of space from both sides of the center of the paper that should be taken up by the heading

23.____

24. You are about to type a single-spaced letter from a typewritten draft. In order to center this letter from top to bottom, your FIRST step should be to
    A. determine the number of spaces needed for the top and bottom margins
    B. determine the number of spaces needed for the left and right margins
    C. count the number of lines, including blank ones, which will be used for the letter
    D. subtract from the number of writing lines on the sheet of paper the number of lines that will not be used for the letter

24.____

25. When typing a table which lists several amounts of money and the total in a column, the dollar sign should be placed in front of the
    A. first dollar amount only
    B. total dollar amount only
    C. first and total dollar amounts only
    D. all of the amounts of money in the column

25.____

26. If a legal document is being prepared and requires necessary information to be typed into blank areas on preprinted legal forms, the margins for a line of typewritten material should be determined PRIMARILY by
    A. counting the total number of words to be typed
    B. the margins set for the pre-printed matter
    C. spacing backwards from the right margin rule
    D. the estimated width and height of the material to be entered

27. When checking for errors in material you've typed, it is BEST to
    A. proofread the material and use the spell-check function in combination
    B. give the material to someone else to review
    C. run the spell-check function and auto-correct all found errors
    D. proofread the material then e-mail it to another typist for final approval

28. Assume that Mr. Frank Foran is an acting official. In a letter written to him, the word *acting* would
    A. be used with the title in the address and in the salutation
    B. not be used with the title in the address
    C. be used with the title in the address but not in the salutation
    D. not be used with the title in the address or in the salutation

29. The software program that requires proficiency in typing in order to best utilize its MOST important features is
    A. Microsoft Excel   B. Adobe Reader
    C. Microsoft Word   D. Intuit QuickBooks

30. The MAIN reason for keeping a careful record of incoming mail is that
    A. greater speed and accuracy is obtained for answering outgoing mail
    B. this record is legal evidence
    C. it develops the efficiency of the office clerks
    D. the information may be useful some day

KEY (CORRECT ANSWERS)

1.	C	11.	C	21.	D
2.	D	12.	D	22.	A
3.	B	13.	D	23.	B
4.	B	14.	B	24.	C
5.	C	15.	D	25.	C
6.	A	16.	B	26.	B
7.	D	17.	C	27.	A
8.	C	18.	A	28.	C
9.	B	19.	B	29.	C
10.	A	20.	C	30.	A

TEST 2

DIRECTIONS: Each question or incomplete statement is followed by several suggested answers or completions. Select the one that BEST answers the question or completes the statement. *PRINT THE LETTER OF THE CORRECT ANSWER IN THE SPACE AT THE RIGHT.*

Questions 1-4.

DIRECTIONS: Questions 1 through 4 are to be answered SOLELY on the basis of the information contained in the following passage which is taken from a typing test.

Modern office methods, geared to ever higher speeds and aimed at ever greater efficiency, are largely the result of the typewriter. The typewriter is a substitute for handwriting; and, in the hands of a skilled typist, not only turns out letters and other documents at least three times faster than a penman can do the work, but turns out the greater volume more uniformly and legibly. With the use of carbon paper and onionskin paper, identical copies can be made at the same time.

The typewriter, besides its effect on the conduct of business and government, has had a very important effect on the position of women. The typewriter has done much to bring women into business and government, and today there are vastly more women than men typists. Many women have used the keys of the typewriter to climb the ladder to responsible managerial positions.

The typewriter, as its name implies, employs type to make an ink impression on paper. For many years, the manual typewriter was the standard machine used. Today, the electric typewriter is dominant, with electronic typewriters, word processors, and computers coming into wider use.

The mechanism of the office manual typewriter includes a set of keys arranged systematically in rows; a semicircular frame of type, connected to the keys by levers; the carriage or paper carrier; a rubber roller called a platen, against which the type strikes; and an inked ribbon which makes the impression of the type character when the key strikes it. This machine, once omnipresent, is an antique today.

1. The above passage mentions a number of good features of the combination of a skilled typist and a typewriter.
   Of the following, the feature which is NOT mentioned in the passage is
   A. speed B. uniformity C. reliability D. legibility

   1.____

2. According to the above passage, a skilled typist can
   A. turn out at least five carbon copies of typed matter
   B. type at least three times faster than a penman can write
   C. type more than 80 words a minute
   D. readily move into a managerial position

   2.____

33

3. According to the above passage, which of the following is NOT part of the mechanism of a manual typewriter?
   A. Carbon paper
   B. Paper carrier
   C. Platen
   D. Inked ribbon

4. According to the above passage, the typewriter has helped
   A. men more than women in business
   B. women in career advancement into management
   C. men and women equally, but women have taken better advantage of it
   D. more women than men, because men generally dislike routine typing work

5. Standard rules for typing spacing have developed through usage. According to these rules, two spaces are left after a(n)
   A. colon
   B. comma
   C. hyphen
   D. opening parenthesis

6. Assume that you have to type the heading CENTERING TYPED HEADINGS on a piece of paper which extends from 0 to 100 on the typewriter scale. You want the heading to be perfectly centered on the paper.
   In order to find the proper point on the typewriter scale at which to begin typing, you should determine the paper's center point on the typewriter scale and then _____ the number of letters and spaces in the heading.
   A. add
   B. add one-half
   C. subtract
   D. subtract one-half

7. While typing from a rough draft, the practice of reading a line ahead of what you are now typing is considered to be a
   A. *good* practice; it may prepare your fingers for the words which you will be typing
   B. *good* practice; it may help you to review the subject matter contained in the material
   C. *poor* practice; it may increase your typing speed so that your accuracy is decreased
   D. *poor* practice; it may cause you to lose your concentration and make errors in the words you are presently typing

8. Assume that you are transcribing a letter and you are not sure how to divide a word at the end of a line you are typing.
   The BEST way to determine where to divide the word is by
   A. asking your supervisor
   B. asking the person who dictated the letter
   C. checking with other stenographers
   D. looking up the word in a dictionary

3 (#2)

9. When taking proper care of a typewriter, it is NOT a desirable action to 9.____
   A. clean the feed rolls with a cloth
   B. dust the exterior surface of the machine
   C. oil the rubber parts of the machine
   D. use a type-cleaning brush to clean the keys

10. Of the following, the LEAST desirable action to take when typing a rough draft of a report is to 10.____
    A. cross out typing errors instead of erasing them
    B. double or triple space between lines
    C. provide large margins on all sides of the typing paper
    D. use letterhead or onionskin paper

11. The date line of every business letter should indicate the month, the day of the month, and the year. 11.____
    The MOST common practice when typing a date line is to type it as
    A. Jan. 12, 2018   B. January 12, 2018
    C. 1-12-18   D. 1/12/18

Questions 12-16.

DIRECTIONS: Questions 12 through 16 are to be answered SOLELY on the basis of the information provided in the following passage.

A written report is a communication of information from one person to another. It is an account of some matter especially investigated, however routine that matter may be. The ultimate basis of any good written report is facts, which became known through observation and verification. Good written reports may seem to be no more than general ideas and opinions. However, in such cases, the facts leading to these opinions were gathered, verified, and reported earlier, and the opinions are dependent upon these facts. Good style, proper form, and emphasis cannot make a good written report out of unreliable information and bad judgments but on the other hand, solid investigation and brilliant thinking are not likely to become very useful until they are effectively communicated to others. If a person's work calls for written reports, then his work is often no better than his written reports.

12. Based on the information in the above passage, it can be concluded that opinions expressed in a report should be 12.____
    A. based on facts which are gathered and reported
    B. emphasized repeatedly when they result from a special investigation
    C. kept to a minimum
    D. separated from the body of the report

13. In the above passage, the one of the following which is mentioned as a way of establishing facts is 13.____
    A. authority   B. communication
    C. reporting   D. verification

14. According to the above passage, the characteristic shared by ALL written reports is that they are
    A. accounts of routine matters
    B. transmissions of information
    C. reliable and logical
    D. written in proper form

15. Which of the following conclusions can LOGICALLY be drawn from the information given in the above passage?
    A. Brilliant thinking can make up for unreliable information in a report.
    B. One method of judging an individual's work is the quality of the written reports he is required to submit.
    C. Proper form and emphasis can make a good report out of unreliable information.
    D. Good written reports that seem to be no more than general ideas should be rewritten.

16. Which of the following suggested titles would be MOST appropriate for this passage?
    A. GATHERING AND ORGANIZING FACTS
    B. TECHNIQUES OF OBSERVATION
    C. NATURE AND PURPOSE OF REPORTS
    D. REPORTS AND OPINIONS: DIFFERENCES AND SIMILARITIES

Questions 17-25

DIRECTIONS: Each of Questions 17 through 25 consists of a sentence which may or may not be an example of good English usage. Examine each sentence, considering grammar, punctuation, spelling, capitalization, and awkwardness. Then choose the correct statement about it from the four choices below it. If the English usage in the sentence given is better than any of the changes suggested in Choices B, C, or D, pick choice A. Do NOT pick a choice that will change the meaning of the sentence.

17. We attended a staff conference on Wednesday the new safety and fire rules were discussed.
    A. This is an example of acceptable writing.
    B. The words *safety*, *fire*, and *rules* should begin with capital letters.
    C. There should be a comma after the word *Wednesday*.
    D. There should be a period after the word *Wednesday*, and the word *the* should begin with a capital letter.

18. Neither the dictionary or the telephone directory could be found in the office library.
    A. This is an example of acceptable writing.
    B. The word *or* should be changed to *nor*.
    C. The word *library* should be spelled *libery*.
    D. The word *neither* should be changed to *either*.

5 (#2)

19. The report would have been typed correctly if the typist cold read the draft. 19.____
    A. This is an example of acceptable writing.
    B. The word *would* should be removed.
    C. The word *have* should be inserted after the word *could*.
    D. The word *correctly* should be changed to *correct*.

20. The supervisor brought the reports and forms to an employees desk. 20.____
    A. This is an example of acceptable writing.
    B. The word *brought* should be changed to *took*.
    C. There should be a comma after the word *reports* and a comma after the word *forms*.
    D. The word *employees* should be spelled *employee's*.

21. It's important for all the office personnel to submit their vacation schedules on time. 21.____
    A. This is an example of acceptable writing.
    B. The word *It's* should be spelled *Its*.
    C. The word *their* should be spelled *they're*.
    D. The word *personnel* should be spelled *personal*.

22. The supervisor wants that all staff members report to the office at 9:00 A.M. 22.____
    A. This is an example of acceptable writing.
    B. The word *that* should be removed and the word *to* should be inserted after the word *members*.
    C. There should be a comma after the word *wants* and a comma after the word *office*.
    D. The word *wants* should be changed to *want* and the word *shall* should be inserted after the word *members*.

23. Every morning the clerk opens the office mail and distributes it. 23.____
    A. This is an example of acceptable writing.
    B. The word *opens* should be changed to *open*.
    C. The word *mail* should be changed to *letters*.
    D. The word *it* should be changed to *them*.

24. The secretary typed more fast on an electric typewriter than on a manual typewriter. 24.____
    A. This is an example of acceptable writing.
    B. The words *more fast* should be changed to *faster*.
    C. There should be a comma after the words *electric typewriter*.
    D. The word *than* should be changed to *then*.

25. The new stenographer needed a desk a typewriter, a chair and a blotter. 25.____
    A. This is an example of acceptable writing.
    B. The word *blotter* should be spelled *blodder*.
    C. The word *stenographer* should begin with a capital letter.
    D. There should be a comma after the word *desk*.

KEY (CORRECT ANSWERS)

1.	C		11.	B
2.	B		12.	A
3.	A		13.	D
4.	B		14.	B
5.	A		15.	B
6.	D		16.	C
7.	D		17.	D
8.	D		18.	B
9.	C		19.	C
10.	D		20.	D

21. A
22. B
23. A
24. B
25. D

EXAMINATION SECTION
TEST 1

DIRECTIONS: Each question or incomplete statement is followed by several suggested answers or completions. Select the one that BEST answers the question or completes the statement. *PRINT THE LETTER OF THE CORRECT ANSWER IN THE SPACE AT THE RIGHT.*

Questions 1-10.

WORD MEANING

DIRECTIONS: Each question from 1 to 10 contains a word in capitals followed by four suggested meanings of the word. For each question, choose the best meaning. *PRINT THE LETTER OF THE CORRECT ANSWER IN THE SPACE AT THE RIGHT.*

1. ACCURATE
   A. correct   B. useful   C. afraid   D. careless

2. ALTER
   A. copy   B. change   C. report   D. agree

3. DOCUMENT
   A. outline   B. agreement   C. blueprint   D. record

4. INDICATE
   A. listen   B. show   C. guess   D. try

5. INVENTORY
   A. custom   B. discovery   C. warning   D. list

6. ISSUE
   A. annoy   B. use up   C. give out   D. gain

7. NOTIFY
   A. inform   B. promise   C. approve   D. strengthen

8. ROUTINE
   A. path   B. mistake   C. habit   D. journey

9. TERMINATE
   A. rest   B. start   C. deny   D. end

10. TRANSMIT
    A. put in   B. send   C. stop   D. go across

Questions 11-15.

READING COMPREHENSION

DIRECTIONS: Questions 11 through 15 test how well you understand what you read. It will be necessary for you to read carefully because your answers to these questions should be based ONLY on the information given in the following paragraphs.

The recipient gains an impression of a typewritten letter before he begins to read the message. Pastors which provide for a good first impression include margins and spacing that are visually pleasing, formal parts of the letter which are correctly placed according to the style of the letter, copy which is free of obvious erasures and over-strikes, and transcript that is even and clear. The problem for the typist is that of how to produce that first, positive impression of her work.

There are several general rules which a typist can follow when she wishes to prepare a properly spaced letter on a sheet of letter-head. Ordinarily, the width of a letter should not be less than four inches nor more than six inches. The side margins should also have a desirable relation to the bottom margin and the space between the letterhead and the body of the letter. Usually the most appealing arrangement is when the side margins are even and the bottom margin is slightly wider than the side margins. In some offices, however, standard line length is used for all business letters, and the secretary then varies the spacing between the date line and the inside address according to the length of the letter.

11. The BEST title for the above paragraphs would be:

    A. Writing Office Letters
    B. Making Good First Impressions
    C. Judging Well-Typed Letters
    D. Good Placing and Spacing for Office Letters

12. According to the above paragraphs, which of the following might be considered the way in which people very quickly judge the quality of work which has been typed? By

    A. measuring the margins to see if they are correct
    B. looking at the spacing and cleanliness of the typescript
    C. scanning the body of the letter for meaning
    D. reading the date line and address for errors

13. What, according to the above paragraphs, would be definitely UNDESIRABLE as the average line length of a typed letter?

    A. 4"   B. 5"   C. 6"   D. 7"

14. According to the above paragraphs, when the line length is kept standard, the secretary

    A. does not have to vary the spacing at all since this also is standard
    B. adjusts the spacing between the date line and inside address for different lengths of letters
    C. uses the longest line as a guideline for spacing between the date line and inside address
    D. varies the number of spaces between the lines

11._____

12._____

13._____

14._____

15. According to the above paragraphs, side margins are MOST pleasing when they   15.____

   A. are even and somewhat smaller than the bottom margin
   B. are slightly wider than the bottom margin
   C. vary with the length of the letter
   D. are figured independently from the letterhead and the body of the letter

Questions 16-20.

CODING

DIRECTIONS:

Name of Applicant	H A N G S B R U K E
Test Code	c o m p l e x i t y
File Number	0 1 2 3 4 5 6 7 8 9

Assume that each of the above capital letters is the first letter of the name of an Applicant, that the small letter directly beneath each capital letter is the test code for the Applicant, and that the number directly beneath each code letter is the file number for the Applicant.

In each of the following Questions 16 through 20, the test code letters and the file numbers in Columns 2 and 3 should correspond to the capital letters in Column 1. For each question, look at each column carefully and mark your answer as follows:

If there is an error only in Column 2, mark your answer A.
If there is an error only in Column 3, mark your answer B.
If there is an error in both Columns 2 and 3, mark your answer C.
If both Columns 2 and 3 are correct, mark your answer D.

The following sample question is given to help you understand the procedure.

SAMPLE QUESTION

Column 1	Column 2	Column 3
AKEHN	otyci	18902

In Column 2, the final test code letter *i.* should be *m*. Column 3 is correctly coded to Column 1. Since there is an error only in Column 2, the answer is A.

	Column 1	Column 2	Column 3	
16.	NEKKU	mytti	29987	16.____
17.	KRAEB	txyle	86095	17.____
18.	ENAUK	ymoit	92178	18.____
19.	REANA	xeomo	69121	19.____
20.	EKHSE	ytcxy	97049	20.____

Questions 21-30.

ARITHMETICAL REASONING

21. If a secretary answered 28 phone calls and typed the addresses for 112 credit statements in one morning, what is the ratio of phone calls answered to credit statements typed for that period of time?

    A. 1:4   B. 1:7   C. 2:3   D. 3:5

22. According to a suggested filing system, no more than 10 folders should be filed behind any one file guide and from 15 to 25 file guides should be used in each file drawer for easy finding and filing.
    The maximum number of folders that a five-drawer file cabinet can hold to allow easy finding and filing is

    A. 550   B. 750   C. 1,100   D. 1,250

23. An employee had a starting salary of $25,804. He received a salary increase at the end of each year, and at the end of the seventh year his salary was $33,476.
    What was his average annual increase in salary over these seven years?

    A. $1,020   B. $1,076   C. $1,096   D. $1,144

24. The 55 typists and 28 senior clerks in a certain city agency were paid a total of $1,943,200 in salaries last year.
    If the average annual salary of a typist was $22,400 the average annual salary of a senior clerk was

    A. $25,400   B. $26,600   C. $26,800   D. $27,000

25. A typist has been given a three page report to type. She has finished typing the first two pages. The first page has 283 words, and the second page has 366 words.
    If the total report consists of 954 words, how many words will she have to type on the third page of the report?

    A. 202   B. 287   C. 305   D. 313

26. In one day, Clerk A processed 30% more forms than Clerk B, and Clerk C processed li times as many forms as Clerk A. If Clerk B processed 40 forms, how many more forms were processed by Clerk C than Clerk B?

    A. 12   B. 13   C. 21   D. 25

27. A clerk who earns a gross salary of $452 every two weeks has the following deductions taken from her paycheck:
    15% for City, State, Federal taxes; 2 1/2% for Social Security; $1.30 for health insurance; and $6.00 for union dues. The amount of her take-home pay is

    A. $256.20   B. $312.40   C. $331.60   D. $365.60

28. In 2005, a city agency spent $2,000 to buy pencils at a cost of $5.00 a dozen.
    If the agency used 3/4 of these pencils in 2005 and used the same number of pencils in 2006, how many more pencils did it have to buy to have enough pencils for all of 2006?

    A. 1,200   B. 2,400   C. 3,600   D. 4,800

5 (#1)

29. A clerk who worked in Agency X earned the following salaries: $20,140 the first year, $21,000 the second year, and $21,920 the third year. Another clerk who worked in Agency Y for three years earned $21,100 a year for two years and $21,448 the third year. The difference between the average salaries received by both clerks over a three-year period is

   A. $196   B. $204   C. $348   D. $564

30. An employee who works over 40 hours in any week receives overtime payment for the extra hours at time and one-half (1 1/2 times) his hourly rate of pay. An employee who earns $13.60 an hour works a total of 45 hours during a certain week.
   His total pay for that week would be

   A. $564.40   B. $612.00   C. $646.00   D. $812.00

Questions 31-35.

RELATED INFORMATION

31. To tell a newly-employed clerk to fill a top drawer of a four-drawer cabinet with heavy folders which will be often used and to keep lower drawers only partly filled is

   A. *good*, because a tall person would have to bend unnecessarily if he had to use a lower drawer
   B. *bad*, because the file cabinet may tip over when the top drawer is opened
   C. *good*, because it is the most easily reachable drawer for the average person
   D. *bad*, because a person bending down at another drawer may accidentally bang his head on the bottom of the drawer when he straightens up

32. If a senior typist or senior clerk has requisitioned a *ream* of paper in order to duplicate a single page office announcement, how many announcements can be printed from the one package of paper?

   A. 200   B. 500   C. 700   D. 1,000

33. Your supervisor has asked you to locate a telephone number for an attorney named Jones, whose office is located at 311 Broadway, and whose name is not already listed in your files.
   The BEST method for finding the number would be for you to

   A. call the information operator and have her get it for you
   B. look in the alphabetical directory (white pages) under the name Jones at 311 Broadway
   C. refer to the heading Attorney in the yellow pages for the name Jones at 311 Broadway
   D. ask your supervisor who referred her to Mr. Jones, then call that person for the number

34. An example of material that should NOT be sent by first class mail is a

   A. email copy of a letter   B. post card
   C. business reply card   D. large catalogue

43

35. In the operations of a government agency, a voucher is ORDINARILY used to 35.____
   A. refer someone to the agency for a position or assignment
   B. certify that an agency's records of financial trans-actions are accurate
   C. order payment from agency funds of a stated amount to an individual
   D. enter a statement of official opinion in the records of the agency

Questions 36-40.

ENGLISH USAGE

DIRECTIONS: Each question from 36 through 40 contains a sentence. Read each sentence carefully to decide whether it is correct. Then, in the space at the right, mark your answer:

(A) if the sentence is incorrect because of bad grammar or sentence structure

(B) if the sentence is incorrect because of bad punctuation

(C) if the sentence is incorrect because of bad capitalization

(D) if the sentence is correct

Each incorrect sentence has only one type of error. Consider a sentence correct if it has no errors, although there may be other correct ways of saying the same thing.

SAMPLE QUESTION I: One of our clerks were promoted yesterday.

The subject of this sentence is *one,* so the verb should be *was promoted* instead of *were promoted.* Since the sentence is incorrect because of bad grammar, the answer to Sample Question I is (A).

SAMPLE QUESTION II: Between you and me, I would prefer not going there.

Since this sentence is correct, the answer to Sample Question II is (D).

36. The National alliance of Businessmen is trying to persuade private businesses to hire youth in the summertime. 36.____

37. The supervisor who is on vacation, is in charge of processing vouchers. 37.____

38. The activity of the committee at its conferences is always stimulating. 38.____

39. After checking the addresses again, the letters went to the mailroom. 39.____

40. The director, as well as the employees, are interested in sharing the dividends. 40.____

Questions 41-45.

FILING

DIRECTIONS: Each question from 41 through 45 contains four names. For each question, choose the name that should be FIRST if the four names are to be arranged in alphabeti-cal order in accordance with the Rules for Alphabetical Filing given below. Read these rules carefully. Then, for each question, indicate in the space at the right the letter before the name that should be FIRST in alphabet-ical order.

RULES FOR ALPHABETICAL FILING

Names of People

(1) The names of people are filed in strict alphabetical order, first according to the last name, then according to first name or initial, and finally according to middle name or initial. FOR EXAMPLE: George Allen comes before Edward Bell, and Leonard P. Reston comes before Lucille B. Reston.

(2) When last names are the same, FOR EXAMPLE, A. Green and Agnes Green, the one with the initial comes before the one with the name written out when the first initials are identi-cal.

(3) When first and last names are alike and the middle name is given, FOR EXAMPLE, John David Doe and John Devoe Doe, the names should be filed in the alphabetical order of the middle names.

(4) When first and last names are the same, a name without a middle initial comes before one with a middle name or initial. FOR EXAMPLE, John Doe comes before both John A. Doe and John Alan Doe.

(5) When first and last names are the same, a name with a middle initial comes before one with a middle name beginning with the same initial. FOR EXAMPLE: Jack R. Hertz comes before Jack Richard Hertz.

(6) Prefixes such as De, O', Mac, Mc, and Van are filed as written and are treated as part of the names to which they are connected. FOR EXAMPLE: Robert O'Dea is filed before David Olsen.

(7) Abbreviated names are treated as if they were spelled out. FOR EXAMPLE: Chas. is filed as Charles and Thos. is filed as Thomas.

(8) Titles and designations such as Dr., Mr., and Prof, are disregarded in filing.

Names of Organizations

(1) The names of business organizations are filed according to the order in which each word in the name appears. When an organization name bears the name of a person, it is filed according to the rules for filing names of people as given above. FOR EXAMPLE: William Smith Service Co. comes before Television Distributors, Inc.

(2) *Where bureau, board, office, or department appears as the first part of the title of a governmental agency, that agency should be filed under the word in the title expressing the chief function of the agency. FOR EXAMPLE: Bureau of the Budget would be filed as if written Budget, (Bureau of the). The Department of Personnel would be filed as if written Personnel, (Department of).*

(3) *When the following words are part of an organization, they are disregarded: the, of, and.*

(4) *When there are numbers in a name, they are treated as if they were spelled out. FOR EXAMPLE: 10th Street Bootery is filed as Tenth Street Bootery.*

SAMPLE QUESTION:
   A. Jane Earl   (2)
   B. James A. Earle   (4)
   C. James Earl   (1)
   D. J. Earle   (3)

The numbers in parentheses show the proper alphabetical order in which these names should be filed. Since the name that should be filed FIRST is James Earl, the answer to the Sample Question is (C).

41.
   A. Majorca Leather Goods
   B. Robert Maiorca and Sons
   C. Maintenance Management Corp.
   D. Majestic Carpet Mills

41.____

42.
   A. Municipal Telephone Service
   B. Municipal Reference Library
   C. Municipal Credit Union
   D. Municipal Broadcasting System

42.____

43.
   A. Robert B. Pierce   B. R. Bruce Pierce
   C. Ronald Pierce   D. Robert Bruce Pierce

43.____

44.
   A. Four Seasons Sports Club   B. 14th. St. Shopping Center
   C. Forty Thieves Restaurant   D. 42nd St. Theaters

44.____

45.
   A. Franco Franceschini   B. Amos Franchini
   C. Sandra Franceschia   D. Lilie Franchinesca

45.____

Questions 46-50.

SPELLING

DIRECTIONS: In each question, one of the words is misspelled. Select the letter of the misspelled word. *PRINT THE LETTER OF THE CORRECT ANSWER IN THE SPACE AT THE RIGHT.*

46.
   A. option   B. extradite
   C. comparitive   D. jealousy

46.____

47.
   A. handicaped   B. assurance
   C. sympathy   D. speech

47.____

48. A. recommend B. carraige 48.____
C. disapprove D. independent

49. A. ingenuity B. tenet (opinion) 49.____
C. uncanny D. intrigueing

50. A. arduous B. hideous 50.____
C. iervant D. companies

KEY (CORRECT ANSWERS)

1. A	11. D	21. A	31. B	41. C
2. B	12. B	22. D	32. B	42. D
3. D	13. D	23. C	33. C	43. B
4. B	14. B	24. A	34. D	44. D
5. D	15. A	25. C	35. C	45. C
6. C	16. B	26. D	36. C	46. C
7. A	17. C	27. D	37. B	47. A
8. C	18. D	28. B	38. D	48. B
9. D	19. A	29. A	39. A	49. D
10. B	20. C	30. C	40. A	50. C

EXAMINATION SECTION
TEST 1

DIRECTIONS: Each question or incomplete statement is followed by several suggested answers or completions. Select the one that BEST answers the question or completes the statement. *PRINT THE LETTER OF THE CORRECT ANSWER IN THE SPACE AT THE RIGHT.*

1. Which of the following is the acceptable format for typing the date line?

   A. 12/2/16
   B. December 2, 2016
   C. December 2nd, 2016
   D. Dec. 2 2016

2. When typing a letter, which of the following is INACCURATE?

   A. If the letter is to be more than one page long, subsequent sheets should be blank, but should match the letterhead sheet in size, color, weight, and texture.
   B. Long quoted material must be centered and single-spaced internally.
   C. Quotation marks must be used when there is long quoted material.
   D. Double spacing is used above and below tables and long quotations to set them off from the rest of the material.

3. Which of the following is INACCURATE?

   A. When an addressee's title in an inside address would overrun the center of a page, it's best to carry part of the title over to another line and to indent it by two spaces.
   B. It is permissible to use ordinal numbers in an inside address.
   C. In addresses involving street numbers under three, the number is written out in full.
   D. In the inside address, suite, apartment or room numbers should be placed on the line after the street address.

4. All of the following are common styles of business letters EXCEPT

   A. simplified
   B. block
   C. direct
   D. executive

5. Please select the two choices below that correctly represent how a continuation sheet heading may be typed.

   I. Page 2
       Mr. Alan Post
       June 25, 2016
   II. Page 2
       Mr. Alan Post
       6-25-16
   III. Mr. Alan Post   -2-
        June 25, 2016
   IV. Mr. Alan Post   -2-
       6-25-16

   The CORRECT answer is:

   A. I, II
   B. II, III
   C. I, III
   D. II, IV

6. Which of the following is INCORRECT? It is

   A. permissible to abbreviate honorifics in the inside address
   B. permissible to abbreviate company or organizational names, departmental designations, or organizational titles in the inside address

C. permissible to use abbreviations in the inside address if they have been used on the printed letterhead and form part of the official company name
D. sometimes permissible to omit the colon after the salutation

7. Which of the following is INCORRECT? 7._____

   A. The subject line of a letter gives the main idea of the message as succinctly as possible.
   B. If a letter contains an enclosure, there should be a notation indicating this.
   C. Important enclosures ought to be listed numerically and described.
   D. An enclosure notation should be typed flush with the right margin.

8. Which of the following is INACCURATE about inside addresses? 8._____

   A. An intraoffice or intracompany mail stop number such as DA 3C 61B is put after the organization or company name with at least two spaces intervening.
   B. Words such as *Avenue* should not be abbreviated.
   C. With the exception of runovers, the inside address should not be more than five full lines.
   D. The inside address includes the recipient's courtesy or honorific title and his or her full name on line one; the recipient's title on the next line; the recipient's official organizational affiliation on the next line; the street address on the penultimate line; and the city, state, and zip code on the last line.

9. Which of the following is an INCORRECT example of how to copy recipients when using copy notation? 9._____

   A. cc: Martin A.Sheen
   B. cc: Ms. Connors
         Ms. Grogan
         Ms. Reynolds
   C. CC: Martin A. Sheen
   D. cc: Mr. Right
         Mr. Wrong
         Mr. Perfect

10. When typing a memo, all of the following are true EXCEPT 10._____

    A. it is permissible to use an abbreviation like 1/1/16
    B. the subject line should be underlined
    C. titles such as *Mr.* or *Dr.* are usually not used on the *To* line
    D. unless the memo is very short, paragraphs should be single-spaced and double spacing should be used to separate the paragraphs from each other

11. When typing a letter, which of the following is INACCURATE? 11._____

    A. Paragraphs in business letters are usually single-spaced, with double spacing separating them from each other.
    B. Margin settings used on subsequent sheets should match those used on the letterhead sheet.
    C. If the message contains an enumerated list, it is best to block and center the listed material by five or six more spaces, right and left.
    D. A quotation of more than three typed lines must be single-spaced and centered on the page.

12. A letter that is to be signed by Hazel Alice Putney, but written by Mary Jane Roberts, and typed by Alice Carol Bell would CORRECTLY bear the following set of initials:

    A. HAP:MJR:acb
    B. HAP:MJR:ab
    C. HAP:mjr:acb
    D. HAP:mjr:ab

13. Which of the following is INCORRECT?

    A. My dear Dr. Jones:
    B. Dear Accounting Department:
    C. Dear Dr. Jones:
    D. Dear Mr. Al Lee, Esq.:

14. Which of the following is INCORRECT?

    A. Bcc stands for blind copy or blind courtesy copy.
    B. When a blind copy is used, the notation bcc appears only on the original.
    C. When a blind copy is used, the notation may appear in the top left corner of the letterhead sheet.
    D. If following a letter style that uses indented paragraphs, the postscript should be indented in exactly the same manner.

15. All of the following are true of the complimentary close EXCEPT

    A. it is typed two lines beneath the last line of the message
    B. when using a minimal punctuation system, you may omit the comma in the complimentary close if you have used a colon in the salutation
    C. where the complimentary close is placed may vary
    D. the first word of the complimentary close is capitalized

16. When typing a letter, which of the following is INACCURATE?

    A. Tables should be centered.
    B. If the letter is to be more than one page long, at least three lines of the message itself should be carried over.
    C. The message begins two lines below the salutation in almost all letter styles.
    D. Triple spacing should be used above and below lists to set them off from the rest of the letter.

17. Which one of the following is INCORRECT?

    A. When used, special mailing instructions should be indicated on both the envelope and the letter itself.
    B. Depending upon the length of the message and the available space, special mailing instructions are usually typed flush left, about four spaces below the date line and about two lines above the first line of the inside address.
    C. Certification, registration, special delivery, and overseas air mail are all considered special mailing instructions.
    D. Special mailing instructions should not be typed in capital letters.

18. Which of the following is INCORRECT?

    A. When a letter is intended to be personal or confidential, these instructions are typewritten in capital letters on the envelope and on the letter itself.

B. When a letter is intended to be personal or confidential, these instructions are typewritten in capital letters on the envelope, but not on the letter.
C. A letter marked PERSONAL is an eyes-only communication for the recipient.
D. A letter marked CONFIDENTIAL means that the recipient and any other authorized person may open and read it.

19. All of the following are true in regard to copy notation EXCEPT 19.____

    A. when included in a letter, a copy notation should be typed flush with the left margin, two lines below the signature block or two lines below any preceding notation
    B. copy notation should appear after writer/typist initials and/or enclosure notations, if these are used
    C. the copy recipient's full name and address should be indicated
    D. if more than one individual is to be copied, recipients should be listed in alphabetical order according to full name or initials

20. When addressing envelopes, which of the following is INACCURATE? 20.____

    A. When both street address and box number are used, the destination of the letter should be placed on the line just above the city, state, and zip code line.
    B. Special mailing instructions are typed in capital letters below the postage.
    C. Special handling instructions should be typed in capital letters and underlined.
    D. The address should be single-spaced.

21. All of the following should be capitalized EXCEPT the 21.____

    A. first word of a direct quotation
    B. first word in the continuation of a split, single-sentence quotation
    C. names of organizations
    D. names of places and geographic districts, regions, divisions, and locales

22. All of the following are true about capitalization EXCEPT 22.____

    A. words indicating direction and regions are capitalized
    B. the names of rivers, seas, lakes, mountains, and oceans are capitalized
    C. the names of nationalities, tribes, languages, and races are capitalized
    D. civil, military, corporate, royal and noble, honorary, and religious titles are capitalized when they precede a name

23. All of the following are true about capitalization EXCEPT 23.____

    A. key words in the titles of musical, dramatic, artistic, and literary works are capitalized as are the first and last words
    B. the first word of the salutation and of the complimentary close of a letter is capitalized
    C. abbreviations and acronyms are not capitalized
    D. the days of the week, months of the year, holidays, and holy days are capitalized

24. All of the following are true EXCEPT 24.____

    A. an apostrophe indicates the omission of letters in contractions
    B. an apostrophe indicates the possessive case of singular and plural nouns

C. an apostrophe should not be used to indicate the omission of figures in dates
D. ellipses are used to indicate the omission of words or sentences within quoted material

25. All of the following are true EXCEPT

    A. brackets may be used to enclose words or passages in quotations to indicate the insertion of material written by someone other than the original writer
    B. brackets may be used to enclose material that is inserted within material already in parentheses
    C. a dash, rather than a colon, should be used to introduce a list
    D. a colon may be used to introduce a long quotation

26. All of the following are true EXCEPT a(n)

    A. comma may be used to set off short quotations and sayings
    B. apostrophe is often used to represent the word *per*
    C. dash may be used to indicate a sudden change or break in continuity
    D. dash may be used to set apart an emphatic or defining phrase

27. All of the following are true EXCEPT

    A. a hyphen may be used as a substitute for the word *to* between figures or words
    B. parentheses are used to enclose material that is not an essential part of the sentence and that, if not included, would not change its meaning
    C. single quotation marks are used to enclose quotations within quotations
    D. semicolons and colons are put inside closing quotation marks

28. All of the following are true EXCEPT

    A. commas and periods should be put inside closing quotation marks
    B. for dramatic effect, a semicolon may be used instead of a comma to signal longer pauses
    C. a semicolon is used to set off city and state in geographic names
    D. italics are used to represent the titles of magazines and newspapers

29. According to standard rules for typing, two spaces are left after a

    A. closing parenthesis   B. comma
    C. number   D. colon

30. All of the following are true EXCEPT

    A. rounding out large numbers is often acceptable
    B. it is best to use numerical figures to express specific hours, measures, dates, page numbers, coordinates, and addresses
    C. when a sentence begins with a number, it is best to use numerical figures rather than to spell the number out
    D. when two or more numbers appear in one sentence, it is best to spell them out consistently or use numerical figures consistently, regardless of the size of the numbers

31. All of the following are true about word division EXCEPT

    A. words should not be divided on a single letter
    B. it is acceptable to carry over two-letter endings
    C. the final word in a paragraph should not be divided
    D. words in headings should not be divided

32. All of the following are true of word division EXCEPT

    A. it is preferable to divide words of three or more syllables after the consonant
    B. it is best to avoid breaking words on more than two consecutive lines
    C. words should be divided according to pronunciation
    D. two-syllable words are divided at the end of the first syllable

33. All of the following are true of word division EXCEPT

    A. words with short prefixes should be divided after the prefix
    B. prefixes and combining forms of more than one syllable should be divided after the first syllable
    C. the following word endings are not divided: -gion, -gious, -sial, -sion, -tial, -tion, -tious, -ceous, -cial, -cient, -cion, -cious, and -geous
    D. words ending in -er should not be divided if the division could only occur on the -er form

34. All of the following are true about word division EXCEPT

    A. words should be divided so that the part of the word left at the end of the line will suggest the word
    B. abbreviations should not be divided
    C. the suffixes -able and -ible are usually divided instead of being carried over intact to the next line
    D. when the addition of -ed, -est, -er, or a similar ending causes the doubling of a final consonant, the added consonant is carried over

35. All of the following are true of word division EXCEPT

    A. words with doubled consonants are usually divided between those consonants
    B. it is permissible to divide contractions
    C. words of one syllable should not be split
    D. it is best to try to avoid divisions that add a hyphen to an already hyphenated word

36. All of the following are true of word division EXCEPT

    A. dividing proper names should be avoided wherever possible
    B. two consonants, preceded and followed by a vowel, are divided after the first consonant
    C. even though two adjoining vowels are sounded separately, it is best not to divide between the two vowels
    D. it is best not to divide the month and day when typing dates, but the year may be carried over to the next line

37. Which of the following four statements are CORRECT? It would be acceptable to divide the word
    I. *organization* after the first *a* in the word
    II. *recommend* after the first *m*
    III. *interface* between the *r* and the *f*
    IV. *development* between the *e* and the *l*
    The CORRECT answer is:

    A. I *only*
    B. II, III
    C. II *only*
    D. I, II, III

38. Which of the following is divided INCORRECTLY?

    A. usu-ally
    B. call-ing
    C. pro-blem
    D. micro-computer

39. Which of the following is divided INCORRECTLY?

    A. imag-inary
    B. commun-ity
    C. manage-able
    D. commun-ion

40. Which of the following is divided INCORRECTLY?

    A. spa-ghetti
    B. retro-spective
    C. proof-reader
    D. fix-ed

41. Which of the following is divided INCORRECTLY?

    A. Mr. Han-rahan
    B. control-lable
    C. pro-jectile
    D. proj-ect

42. Which of the following is divided INCORRECTLY?

    A. prom-ise
    B. han-dling
    C. have-n't
    D. pro-duce

43. Which of the following is divided INCORRECTLY?

    A. ship-ped
    B. audi-ble
    C. hypo-crite
    D. refer-ring

44. Which of the following is divided INCORRECTLY?

    A. particu-lar
    B. spac-ious
    C. chang-ing
    D. capac-ity

45. There is a critical need to develop the ability to control the mind, especailly the ability to stop repeating negative thoughts. Often, when we must swallow our anger, we are left running an enless tape of thoughts. We can't stop thinking about what the person said and what we should have said in response. To combat this tendency, it is helpful to practice witnessing our thoughts. If we can remain detached from them, we won't fuel them, and they will just run out of gas. As we watch them, we also learn a lot about ourselves. The catch here is not to judge them. Judging may lead to selfblaming, blaming others, excuses, rationalizations, and other thoughts that just add fuel. Another technique is is substituting positive thoughts for negative ones.

8 (#1)

It is difficult to do this in the "heat of the moment". With practice, however, its possible to train the mind to do what we want it to do and to contain what we want it to contain.
A mind is like a garden – we can weed it, or we can let it grow wild.
The above paragraph contains a number of typographical errors.
How many lines in this paragraph contain typographical errors?

A. 5   B. 6   C. 8   D. 9

KEY (CORRECT ANSWERS)

1. B	11. D	21. B	31. B	41. A
2. C	12. A	22. A	32. A	42. A
3. D	13. D	23. C	33. B	43. A
4. C	14. B	24. C	34. C	44. B
5. C	15. B	25. C	35. B	45. C
6. B	16. D	26. B	36. C	
7. D	17. D	27. D	37. B	
8. B	18. B	28. C	38. C	
9. D	19. C	29. D	39. B	
10. B	20. C	30. C	40. D	

TEST 2

DIRECTIONS: Each sentence may or may not contain problems in capitalization or punctuation. If there is an error, select the number of the underlined part that must be changed to make the sentence correct. If the sentence has no error, select choice E. <u>No sentence contains more than one error.</u>

1. Is the choice for <u>P</u>resident of the company<u>, George Dawson,</u> or Marilyn Kappel<u>?</u> <u>No error</u>
               A   B   C   D   E

1._____

2. "To tell you the truth<u>,</u> I was really <u>disappointed that</u> our <u>F</u>all percentages did not show more sales growth<u>,</u>" remarked the bookkeeper. <u>No error</u>
      A   B   C   D   E

2._____

3. Bruce gave his <u>U</u>ncle clear directions to go <u>s</u>outh on Maplewood Drive<u>,</u> turn left at the intersection with Birch Lane, and then proceed for two miles until he reached Columbia <u>C</u>ounty. <u>No error</u>
          A   B   C   D   E

3._____

4. Janet hopes to transfer to a <u>c</u>ollege in the <u>e</u>ast <u>d</u>uring her <u>j</u>unior year. <u>No error</u>
                                 A   B C   D   E

4._____

5. The <u>D</u>eclaration <u>o</u>f Independence states <u>that</u> we have the right to the pursuit of <u>H</u>appiness, but it doesn't guarantee that we'll ever find it. <u>No error</u>
     A   B   C   D   E

5._____

6. We campaigned hard for the <u>mayor,</u> but <u>we'</u>re still not sure if he'll win against <u>S</u>enator Frankovich. <u>No error</u>
                                A B C   D   E

6._____

7. Mr. <u>Butler'</u>s <u>F</u>ord was parked right behind <u>our's</u> on Atlantic <u>A</u>venue. <u>No error</u>
       A B   C   D   E

7._____

8. "<u>I</u> respect your <u>opinion,</u> but I cannot agree with <u>it."</u> commented my <u>g</u>randmother. <u>No error</u>
   A   B   C   D   E

8._____

2 (#2)

9. My friends, of course, were surprised when when I did so well on the Math section
      A   B   C   D
of the test. No error
              E

10. Dr. Vogel and Senator Rydell decided that the meeting would be held on February 6,
              A   B   C
in Ithaca, New York. No error
      D   E

11. "Frank, do you understand what we're telling you?" asked the doctor. No error
         A   B   C   D   E

12. When I asked my daughter what she knew about politics, she claimed she
                       A   B   C
knew nothing. No error
         D   E

13. "If you went to my high school, dad, you'd see things differently," snapped Sean.
                         A   A   B C   D
No error
   E

14. In Carlos' third year of high school, he took geometry, psychology, french, and chemis-
         A   B   B   C   D
try. No error
         E

15. "When you enter the building," the guard instructed us, "turn left down the long, wind-
                              A   B C   D
ing corridor." No error
                      E

16. We hope to spend a weekend in the Catskill Mountains in the spring, and we'd like to
                                                 A   B   C   D
go to Florida in January. No error
                                E

17. A clerk in the department of Justice asked Carol and me if we were there on business or
       A   B   C
just sight-seeing. No error
              D   E

18. Jamie joined a cult, Harry's in a rock band, and Carol-Ann is studying chinese literature   18.____
          A   B   C
    at the University of Southern California. No error
             D   E

19. Parker Flash asked if my band had ever played at the   19.____
                      A
    Purple Turnip, a club in Orinoco Hills. No error
    B   C   D   E

20. "The gift of the Magi" is a short story by O'Henry that deals with the sad ironies of life.   20.____
         A B C   D
    No error
    E

21. Darwin's theory was developed, as a result of his trip to the Galapagos Islands.   21.____
        A B   C   D
    No error
    E

22. Is 10 Downing street the address of Sherlock Holmes or the British Prime Minister?   22.____
            A   B   C   D
    No error
    E

23. While President Johnson was in Office, his Great Society program passed a great deal   23.____
              A   B   C   D
    of important legislation. No error
                              E

24. If, as the American Industrial Health Council's study says, one out of every five can-   24.____
        A   B   C
    cers today is caused by the workplace, it is a tragic indictment of what is happening
                                D
    there. No error
           E

25. According to the Articles of Confederation, Congress could issue money, but it could   25.____
                                A   B   C
    not prevent States from issuing their own money. No error
                   D   E

4 (#2)

26. "I'd really like to know whos going to be shoveling the driveway this winter," said
        A   B   C   D
    Laverne. No error
             E

27. According to Carl Jung the Swiss psychologist, playing with fantasy is the key to cre-
                         A   B   C   D
    ativity. No error
            E

28. Don't you find it odd that people would prefer jumping A off the Golden Gate bridge to
        A   B
    jumping off other bridges in the area ? No error
                                    C   D   E

29. While driving through the South, we saw many of the sites of famous Civil war battles.
                                A   B   C   D
    No error
    E

30. Although I have always valued my Grandmother's china, I prefer her collection
                                          A   B   C
    of South American art. No error
       D   E

60

KEY (CORRECT ANSWERS)

1.	A		16.	E
2.	C		17.	B
3.	A		18.	C
4.	B		19.	C
5.	D		20.	A
6.	E		21.	C
7.	C		22.	B
8.	E		23.	B
9.	D		24.	D
10.	E		25.	D
11.	A		26.	B
12.	B		27.	A
13.	C		28.	B
14.	D		29.	C
15.	E		30.	A

RECORD KEEPING
EXAMINATION SECTION
TEST 1

DIRECTIONS: Each question or incomplete statement is followed by several suggested answers or completions. Select the one that BEST answers the question or completes the statement. *PRINT THE LETTER OF THE CORRECT ANSWER IN THE SPACE AT THE RIGHT.*

Questions 1-15.

DIRECTIONS: Questions 1 through 15 are to be answered on the basis of the following list of company names below. Arrange a file alphabetically, word-by-word, disregarding punctuation, conjunctions, and apostrophes. Then answer the questions.

A Bee C Reading Materials
ABCO Parts
A Better Course for Test Preparation
AAA Auto Parts Co.
A-Z Auto Parts, Inc.
Aabar Books
Abbey, Joanne
Boman-Sylvan Law Firm
BMW Autowerks
C Q Service Company
Chappell-Murray, Inc.
E&E Life Insurance
Emcrisco
Gigi Arts
Gordon, Jon & Associates
SOS Plumbing
Schmidt, J.B. Co.

1. Which of these files should appear FIRST?

    A. ABCO Parts
    B. A Bee C Reading Materials
    C. A Better Course for Test Preparation
    D. AAA Auto Parts Co.

1._____

2. Which of these files should appear SECOND?

    A. A-Z Auto Parts, Inc.
    B. A Bee C Reading Materials
    C. A Better Course for Test Preparation
    D. AAA Auto Parts Co.

2._____

3. Which of these files should appear THIRD?

    A. ABCO Parts
    B. A Bee C Reading Materials
    C. Aabar Books
    D. AAA Auto Parts Co.

3._____

4. Which of these files should appear FOURTH?

   A. Aabar Books
   B. ABCO Parts
   C. Abbey, Joanne
   D. AAA Auto Parts Co.

5. Which of these files should appear LAST?

   A. Gordon, Jon & Associates
   B. Gigi Arts
   C. Schmidt, J.B. Co.
   D. SOS Plumbing

6. Which of these files should appear between A-Z Auto Parts, Inc. and Abbey, Joanne?

   A. A Bee C Reading Materials
   B. AAA Auto Parts Co.
   C. ABCO Parts
   D. A Better Course for Test Preparation

7. Which of these files should appear between ABCO Parts and Aabar Books?

   A. A Bee C Reading Materials
   B. Abbey, Joanne
   C. Aabar Books
   D. A-Z Auto Parts

8. Which of these files should appear between Abbey, Joanne and Boman-Sylvan Law Firm?

   A. A Better Course for Test Preparation
   B. BMW Autowerks
   C. Chappell-Murray, Inc.
   D. Aabar Books

9. Which of these files should appear between Abbey, Joanne and C Q Service?

   A. A-Z Auto Parts,Inc.
   B. BMW Autowerks
   C. Choices A and B
   D. Chappell-Murray, Inc.

10. Which of these files should appear between C Q Service Company and Emcrisco?

    A. Chappell-Murray, Inc.
    B. E&E Life Insurance
    C. Gigi Arts
    D. Choices A and B

11. Which of these files should NOT appear between C Q Service Company and E&E Life Insurance?

    A. Gordon, Jon & Associates
    B. Emcrisco
    C. Gigi Arts
    D. All of the above

12. Which of these files should appear between Chappell-Murray Inc., and Gigi Arts? 12.____

    A. CQ Service Inc. E&E Life Insurance, and Emcrisco
    B. Emcrisco, E&E Life Insurance, and Gordon, Jon & Associates
    C. E&E Life Insurance and Emcrisco
    D. Emcrisco and Gordon, Jon & Associates

13. Which of these files should appear between Gordon, Jon & Associates and SOS Plumbing? 13.____

    A. Gigi Arts   B. Schmidt, J.B. Co.
    C. Choices A and B   D. None of the above

14. Each of the choices lists the four files in their proper alphabetical order except 14.____

    A. E&E Life Insurance; Gigi Arts; Gordon, Jon & Associates; SOS Plumbing
    B. E&E Life Insurance; Emcrisco; Gigi Arts; SOS Plumbing
    C. Emcrisco; Gordon, Jon & Associates; SOS Plumbing; Schmidt, J.B. Co.
    D. Emcrisco; Gigi Arts; Gordon, Jon & Associates; SOS Plumbing

15. Which of the choices lists the four files in their proper alphabetical order? 15.____

    A. Gigi Arts; Gordon, Jon & Associates; SOS Plumbing; Schmidt, J.B. Co.
    B. Gordon, Jon & Associates; Gigi Arts; Schmidt, J.B. Co.; SOS Plumbing
    C. Gordon, Jon & Associates; Gigi Arts; SOS Plumbing; Schmidt, J.B. Co.
    D. Gigi Arts; Gordon, Jon & Associates; Schmidt, J.B. Co.; SOS Plumbing

16. The alphabetical filing order of two businesses with identical names is determined by the 16.____

    A. length of time each business has been operating
    B. addresses of the businesses
    C. last name of the company president
    D. none of the above

17. In an alphabetical filing system, if a business name includes a number, it should be 17.____

    A. disregarded
    B. considered a number and placed at the end of an alphabetical section
    C. treated as though it were written in words and alphabetized accordingly
    D. considered a number and placed at the beginning of an alphabetical section

18. If a business name includes a contraction (such as *don't* or *it's*), how should that word be treated in an alphabetical filing system? 18.____

    A. Divide the word into its separate parts and treat it as two words.
    B. Ignore the letters that come after the apostrophe.
    C. Ignore the word that contains the contraction.
    D. Ignore the apostrophe and consider all letters in the contraction.

19. In what order should the parts of an address be considered when using an alphabetical filing system? 19.____

    A. City or town; state; street name; house or building number
    B. State; city or town; street name; house or building number
    C. House or building number; street name; city or town; state
    D. Street name; city or town; state

20. A business record should be cross-referenced when a(n)

   A. organization is known by an abbreviated name
   B. business has a name change because of a sale, incorporation, or other reason
   C. business is known by a *coined* or common name which differs from a dictionary spelling
   D. all of the above

21. A geographical filing system is MOST effective when

   A. location is more important than name
   B. many names or titles sound alike
   C. dealing with companies who have offices all over the world
   D. filing personal and business files

Questions 22-25.

DIRECTIONS: Questions 22 through 25 are to be answered on the basis of the list of items below, which are to be filed geographically. Organize the items geographically and then answer the questions.
  1. University Press at Berkeley, U.S.
  2. Maria Sanchez, Mexico City, Mexico
  3. Great Expectations Ltd. in London, England
  4. Justice League, Cape Town, South Africa, Africa
  5. Crown Pearls Ltd. in London, England
  6. Joseph Prasad in London, England

22. Which of the following arrangements of the items is composed according to the policy of: *Continent, Country, City, Firm or Individual Name?*

   A. 5, 3, 4, 6, 2, 1   B. 4, 5, 3, 6, 2, 1
   C. 1, 4, 5, 3, 6, 2   D. 4, 5, 3, 6, 1, 2

23. Which of the following files is arranged according to the policy of: *Continent, Country, City, Firm or Individual Name?*

   A. South Africa. Africa. Cape Town. Justice League
   B. Mexico. Mexico City, Maria Sanchez
   C. North America. United States. Berkeley. University Press
   D. England. Europe. London. Prasad, Joseph

24. Which of the following arrangements of the items is composed according to the policy of: *Country, City, Firm or Individual Name?*

   A. 5, 6, 3, 2, 4, 1   B. 1, 5, 6, 3, 2, 4
   C. 6, 5, 3, 2, 4, 1   D. 5, 3, 6, 2, 4, 1

25. Which of the following files is arranged according to a policy of: *Country, City, Firm or Individual Name?*

   A. England. London. Crown Pearls Ltd.
   B. North America. United States. Berkeley. University Press
   C. Africa. Cape Town. Justice League
   D. Mexico City. Mexico. Maria Sanchez

26. Under which of the following circumstances would a phonetic filing system be MOST effective?   26._____

    A. When the person in charge of filing can't spell very well
    B. With large files with names that sound alike
    C. With large files with names that are spelled alike
    D. All of the above

Questions 27-29.

DIRECTIONS: Questions 27 through 29 are to be answered on the basis of the following list of numerical files.
    1. 391-023-100
    2. 361-132-170
    3. 385-732-200
    4. 381-432-150
    5. 391-632-387
    6. 361-423-303
    7. 391-123-271

27. Which of the following arrangements of the files follows a consecutive-digit system?   27._____

    A. 2, 3, 4, 1   B. 1, 5, 7, 3
    C. 2, 4, 3, 1   D. 3, 1, 5, 7

28. Which of the following arrangements follows a terminal-digit system?   28._____

    A. 1, 7, 2, 4, 3   B. 2, 1, 4, 5, 7
    C. 7, 6, 5, 4, 3   D. 1, 4, 2, 3, 7

29. Which of the following lists follows a middle-digit system?   29._____

    A. 1, 7, 2, 6, 4, 5, 3   B. 1, 2, 7, 4, 6, 5, 3
    C. 7, 2, 1, 3, 5, 6, 4   D. 7, 1, 2, 4, 6, 5, 3

Questions 30-31.

DIRECTIONS: Questions 30 and 31 are to be answered on the basis of the following information.
    1. Reconfirm Laura Bates appointment with James Caldecort on December 12 at 9:30 A.M.
    2. Laurence Kinder contact Julia Lucas on August 3 and set up a meeting for week of September 23 at 4 P.M.
    3. John Lutz contact Larry Waverly on August 3 and set up appointment for September 23 at 9:30 A.M.
    4. Call for tickets for Gerry Stanton August 21 for New Jersey on September 23, flight 143 at 4:43 P.M.

30. A chronological file for the above information would be 30._____

   A. 4, 3, 2, 1 B. 3, 2, 4, 1
   C. 4, 2, 3, 1 D. 3, 1, 2, 4

31. Using the above information, a chronological file for the date of September 23 would be 31._____

   A. 2, 3, 4   B. 3, 1, 4   C. 3, 2, 4   D. 4, 3, 2

Questions 32-34.

   DIRECTIONS: Questions 32 through 34 are to be answered on the basis of the following information.
   1. Call Roger Epstein, Ashoke Naipaul, Jon Anderson, and Sarah Washington on April 19 at 1:00 P.M. to set up meeting with Alika D'Ornay for June 6 in New York.
   2. Call Martin Ames before noon on April 19 to confirm afternoon meeting with Bob Greenwood on April 20th
   3. Set up meeting room at noon for 2:30 P.M. meeting on April 19th;
   4. Ashley Stanton contact Bob Greenwood at 9:00 A.M. on April 20 and set up meeting for June 6 at 8:30 A.M.
   5. Carol Guiland contact Shelby Van Ness during afternoon of April 20 and set up meeting for June 6 at 10:00 A.M.
   6. Call airline and reserve tickets on June 6 for Roger Epstein trip *to* Denver on July 8
   7. Meeting at 2:30 P.M. on April 19th

32. A chronological file for all of the above information would be 32._____

   A. 2, 1, 3, 7, 5, 4, 6   B. 3, 7, 2, 1, 4, 5, 6
   C. 3, 7, 1, 2, 5, 4, 6   D. 2, 3, 1, 7, 4, 5, 6

33. A chronological file for the date of April 19th would be 33._____

   A. 2, 3, 7, 1   B. 2, 3, 1, 7
   C. 7, 1, 3, 2   D. 3, 7, 1, 2

34. Add the following information to the file, and then create a chronological file for April 20th: 34._____
    8. April 20: 3:00 P.M. meeting between Bob Greenwood and Martin Ames.

   A. 4, 5, 8   B. 4, 8, 5   C. 8, 5, 4   D. 5, 4, 8

35. The PRIMARY advantage of computer records filing over a manual system is 35._____

   A. speed of retrieval   B. accuracy
   C. cost   D. potential file loss

KEY (CORRECT ANSWERS)

1.	B		16.	B
2.	C		17.	C
3.	D		18.	D
4.	A		19.	A
5.	D		20.	D
6.	C		21.	A
7.	B		22.	B
8.	B		23.	C
9.	C		24.	D
10.	D		25.	A
11.	D		26.	B
12.	C		27.	C
13.	B		28.	D
14.	C		29.	A
15.	D		30.	B

31. C
32. D
33. B
34. A
35. A

EXAMINATION SECTION
TEST 1

DIRECTIONS: In each of the following questions, only one of the four sentences conforms to standards of correct usage. The other three contain errors in grammar, diction, or punctuation. Select the choice in each question which BEST conforms to standards of correct usage. Consider a choice correct if it contains none of the errors mentioned above, even though there may be other ways of expressing the same thought. *PRINT THE LETTER OF THE CORRECT ANSWER IN THE SPACE AT THE RIGHT.*

1.
   A. Because he was ill was no excuse for his behavior.
   B. I insist that he see a lawyer before he goes to trial.
   C. He said "that he had not intended to go."
   D. He wasn't out of the office only three days.

   1.____

2.
   A. He came to the station and pays a porter to carry his bags into the train.
   B. I should have liked to live in medieval times.
   C. My father was born in Linville. A little country town where everyone knows everyone else.
   D. The car, which is parked across the street, is disabled.

   2.____

3.
   A. He asked the desk clerk for a clean, quiet, room.
   B. I expected James to be lonesome and that he would want to go home.
   C. I have stopped worrying because I have heard nothing further on the subject.
   D. If the board of directors controls the company, they may take actions which are disapproved by the stockholders.

   3.____

4.
   A. Each of the players knew their place.
   B. He whom you saw on the stage is the son of an actor.
   C. Susan is the smartest of the twin sisters.
   D. Who ever thought of him winning both prizes?

   4.____

5.
   A. An outstanding trait of early man was their reliance on omens.
   B. Because I had never been there before.
   C. Neither Mr. Jones nor Mr. Smith has completed his work.
   D. While eating my dinner, a dog came to the window.

   5.____

6.
   A. A copy of the lease, in addition to the Rules and Regulations, are to be given to each tenant.
   B. The Rules and Regulations and a copy of the lease is being given to each tenant.
   C. A copy of the lease, in addition to the Rules and Regulations, is to be given to each tenant.
   D. A copy of the lease, in addition to the Rules and Regulations, are being given to each tenant.

   6.____

7.
   A. Although we understood that for him music was a passion, we were disturbed by the fact that he was addicted to sing along with the soloists.
   B. Do you believe that Steven is liable to win a scholarship?
   C. Give the picture to whomever is a connoisseur of art.
   D. Whom do you believe to be the most efficient worker in the office?

   7.____

8. A. Each adult who is sure they know all the answers will some day realize their mistake.
    B. Even the most hardhearted villain would have to feel bad about so horrible a tragedy.
    C. Neither being licensed teachers, both aspirants had to pass rigorous tests before being appointed.
    D. The principal reason why he wanted to be designated was because he had never before been to a convention.

8.____

9. A. Being that the weather was so inclement, the party has been postponed for at least a month.
    B. He is in New York City only three weeks and he has already seen all the thrilling sights in Manhattan and in the other four boroughs.
    C. If you will look it up in the official directory, which can be consulted in the library during specified hours, you will discover that the chairman and director are Mr. T. Henry Long.
    D. Working hard at college during the day and at the post office during the night, he appeared to his family to be indefatigable.

9.____

10. A. I would have been happy to oblige you if you only asked me to do it.
    B. The cold weather, as well as the unceasing wind and rain, have made us decide to spend the winter in Florida.
    C. The politician would have been more successful in winning office if he would have been less dogmatic.
    D. These trousers are expensive; however, they will wear well.

10.____

11. A. All except him wore formal attire at the reception for the ambassador.
    B. If that chair were to be blown off of the balcony, it might injure someone below.
    C. Not a passenger, who was in the crash, survived the impact.
    D. To borrow money off friends is the best way to lose them.

11.____

12. A. Approaching Manhattan on the ferry boat from Staten Island, an unforgettable sight of the skyscrapers is seen.
    B. Did you see the exhibit of modernistic paintings as yet?
    C. Gesticulating wildly and ranting in stentorian tones, the speaker was the sinecure of all eyes.
    D. The airplane with crew and passengers was lost somewhere in the Pacific Ocean.

12.____

13. A. If one has consistently had that kind of training, it is certainly too late to change your entire method of swimming long distances.
    B. The captain would have been more impressed if you would have been more conscientious in evacuation drills.
    C. The passengers on the stricken ship were all ready to abandon it at the signal.
    D. The villainous shark lashed at the lifeboat with it's tail, trying to upset the rocking boat in order to partake of it's contents.

13.____

14. A. As one whose been certified as a professional engineer, I believe that the decision to build a bridge over that harbor is unsound.
    B. Between you and me, this project ought to be completed long before winter arrives.
    C. He fervently hoped that the men would be back at camp and to find them busy at their usual chores.
    D. Much to his surprise, he discovered that the climate of Korea was like his home town.

14._____

15. A. An industrious executive is aided, not impeded, by having a hobby which gives him a fresh point of view on life and its problems.
    B. Frequent absence during the calendar year will surely mitigate against the chances of promotion.
    C. He was unable to go to the committee meeting because he was very ill.
    D. Mr. Brown expressed his disapproval so emphatically that his associates were embarassed.

15._____

16. A. At our next session, the office manager will have told you something about his duties and responsibilities.
    B. In general, the book is absorbing and original and have no hesitation about recommending it.
    C. The procedures followed by private industry in dealing with lateness and absence are different from ours.
    D. We shall treat confidentially any information about Mr. Doe, to whom we understand you have sent reports to for many years.

16._____

17. A. I talked to one official, whom I knew was fully impartial.
    B. Everyone signed the petition but him.
    C. He proved not only to be a good student but also a good athlete.
    D. All are incorrect.

17._____

18. A. Every year a large amount of tenants are admitted to housing projects.
    B. Henry Ford owned around a billion dollars in industrial equipment.
    C. He was aggravated by the child's poor behavior.
    D. All are incorrect.

18._____

19. A. Before he was committed to the asylum he suffered from the illusion that he was Napoleon.
    B. Besides stocks, there were also bonds in the safe.
    C. We bet the other team easily.
    D. All are incorrect.

19._____

20. A. Bring this report to your supervisor immediately.
    B. He set the chair down near the table.
    C. The capitol of New York is Albany.
    D. All are incorrect.

20._____

21. A. He was chosen to arbitrate the dispute because everyone knew he would be disinterested.
    B. It is advisable to obtain the best council before making an important decision.
    C. Less college students are interested in teaching than ever before.
    D. All are incorrect.

21._____

22. A. She, hearing a signal, the source lamp flashed.   22.____
     B. While hearing a signal, the source lamp flashed.
     C. In hearing a signal, the source lamp flashed.
     D. As she heard a signal, the source lamp flashed.

23. A. Every one of the time records have been initialed in the designated spaces.   23.____
     B. All of the time records has been initialed in the designated spaces.
     C. Each one of the time records was initialed in the designated spaces.
     D. The time records all been initialed in the designated spaces.

24. A. If there is no one else to answer the phone, you will have to answer it.   24.____
     B. You will have to answer it yourself if no one else answers the phone.
     C. If no one else is not around to pick up the phone, you will have to do it.
     D. You will have to answer the phone when nobodys here to do it.

25. A. Dr. Barnes not in his office. What could I do for you?   25.____
     B. Dr. Barnes is not in his office. Is there something I can do for you?
     C. Since Dr. Barnes is not in his office, might there be something I may do for you?
     D. Is there any ways I can assist you since Dr. Barnes is not in his office?

26. A. She do not understand how the new console works.   26.____
     B. The way the new console works, she doesn't understand.
     C. She doesn't understand how the new console works.
     D. The new console works, so that she doesn't understand.

27. A. Certain changes in family income must be reported as they occur.   27.____
     B. When certain changes in family income occur, it must be reported.
     C. Certain family income changes must be reported as they occur.
     D. Certain changes in family income must be reported as they have been occuring.

28. A. Each tenant has to complete the application themselves.   28.____
     B. Each of the tenants have to complete the application by himself.
     C. Each of the tenants has to complete the application himself.
     D. Each of the tenants has to complete the application by themselves.

29. A. Yours is the only building that the construction will effect.   29.____
     B. Your's is the only building affected by the construction.
     C. The construction will only effect your building.
     D. Yours is the only building that will be affected by the construction.

30. A. There is four tests left.   30.____
     B. The number of tests left are four.
     C. There are four tests left.
     D. Four of the tests remains.

31. A. Each of the applicants takes a test.   31.____
     B. Each of the applicants take a test.
     C. Each of the applicants take tests.
     D. Each of the applicants have taken tests.

32. A. The applicant, not the examiners, are ready.
     B. The applicants, not the examiner, is ready.
     C. The applicants, not the examiner, are ready.
     D. The applicant, not the examiner, are ready.

33. A. You will not progress except you practice.
     B. You will not progress without you practicing.
     C. You will not progress unless you practice.
     D. You will not progress provided you do not practice.

34. A. Neither the director or the employees will be at the office tomorrow.
     B. Neither the director nor the employees will be at the office tomorrow.
     C. Neither the director, or the secretary nor the other employees will be at the office tomorrow.
     D. Neither the director, the secretary or the other employees will be at the office tomorrow.

35. A. In my absence he and her will have to finish the assignment.
     B. In my absence he and she will have to finish the assignment.
     C. In my absence she and him, they will have to finish the assignment.
     D. In my absence he and her both will have to finish the assignment.

KEY (CORRECT ANSWERS)

1.	B	16.	C
2.	B	17.	B
3.	C	18.	D
4.	B	19.	B
5.	C	20.	B
6.	C	21.	A
7.	D	22.	D
8.	B	23.	C
9.	D	24.	A
10.	D	25.	B
11.	A	26.	C
12.	D	27.	A
13.	C	28.	C
14.	B	29.	D
15.	A	30.	C

31. A
32. C
33. C
34. B
35. B

TEST 2

DIRECTIONS: Each question or incomplete statement is followed by several suggested answers or completions. Select the one that BEST answers the question or completes the statement. *PRINT THE LETTER OF THE CORRECT ANSWER IN THE SPACE AT THE RIGHT.*

Questions 1-4.

DIRECTIONS: Questions 1 through 4 consist of three sentences each. For each question, select the sentence which contains NO error in grammar or usage.

1. A. Be sure that everybody brings his notes to the conference. 1.____
    B. He looked like he meant to hit the boy.
    C. Mr. Jones is one of the clients who was chosen to represent the district
    D. All are incorrect.

2. A. He is taller than I. 2.____
    B. I'll have nothing to do with these kind of people.
    C. The reason why he will not buy the house is because it is too expensive.
    D. All are incorrect.

3. A. Aren't I eligible for this apartment. 3.____
    B. Have you seen him anywheres?
    C. He should of come earlier.
    D. All are incorrect.

4. A. He graduated college in 1982. 4.____
    B. He hadn't but one more line to write.
    C. Who do you think is the author of this report?
    D. All are incorrect.

Questions 5-35.

DIRECTIONS: In each of the following questions, only one of the four sentences conforms to standards of correct usage. The other three contain errors in grammar, diction, or punctuation. Select the choice in each question which BEST conforms to standards of correct usage. Consider a choice correct if it contains none of the errors mentioned above, even though there may be other ways of expressing the same thought.

5. A. It is obvious that no one wants to be a kill-joy if they can help it. 5.____
    B. It is not always possible, and perhaps it never ispossible, to judge a person's character by just looking at him.
    C. When Yogi Berra of the New York Yankees hit an immortal grandslam home run, everybody in the huge stadium including Pittsburgh fans, rose to his feet.
    D. Every one of us students must pay tuition today.

6. A. The physician told the young mother that if the baby is not able to digest its milk, it should be boiled.
    B. There is no doubt whatsoever that he felt deeply hurt because John Smith had betrayed the trust.
    C. Having partaken of a most delicious repast prepared by Tessie Breen, the hostess, the horses were driven home immediately thereafter.
    D. The attorney asked my wife and myself several questions.

6.____

7. A. Despite all denials, there is no doubt in my mind that
    B. At this time everyone must deprecate the demogogic attack made by one of our Senators on one of our most revered statesmen.
    C. In the first game of a crucial two-game series, Ted Williams, got two singles, both of them driving in a run.
    D. Our visitor brought good news to John and I.

7.____

8. A. If he would have told me, I should have been glad to help him in his dire financial emergency.
    B. Newspaper men have often asserted that diplomats or so-called official spokesmen sometimes employ equivocation in attempts to deceive.
    C. I think someones coming to collect money for the Red Cross.
    D. In a masterly summation, the young attorney expressed his belief that the facts clearly militate against this opinion.

8.____

9. A. We have seen most all the exhibits.
    B. Without in the least underestimating your advice, in my opinion the situation has grown immeasurably worse in the past few days.
    C. I wrote to the box office treasurer of the hit show that a pair of orchestra seats would be preferable.
    D. As the grim story of Pearl Harbor was broadcast on that fateful December 7, it was the general opinion that war was inevitable.

9.____

10. A. Without a moment's hesitation, Casey Stengel said that Larry Berra works harder than any player on the team.
    B. There is ample evidence to indicate that many animals can run faster than any human being.
    C. No one saw the accident but I.
    D. Example of courage is the heroic defense put up by the paratroopers against overwhelming odds.

10.____

11. A. If you prefer these kind, Mrs. Grey, we shall be more than willing to let you have them reasonably.
    B. If you like these here, Mrs. Grey, we shall be more than willing to let you have them reasonably.
    C. If you like these, Mrs. Grey, we shall be more than willing to let you have them.
    D. Who shall we appoint?

11.____

12. A. The number of errors are greater in speech than in writing.
    B. The doctor rather than the nurse was to blame for his being neglected.
    C. Because the demand for these books have been so great, we reduced the price.
    D. John Galsworthy, the English novelist, could not have survived a serious illness; had it not been for loving care.

12.____

13. A. Our activities this year have seldom ever been as interesting as they have been this month. 13.____
    B. Our activities this month have been more interesting, or at least as interesting as those of any month this year.
    C. Our activities this month has been more interesting than those of any other month this year.
    D. Neither Jean nor her sister was at home.

14. A. George B. Shaw's view of common morality, as well as his wit sparkling with a dash of perverse humor here and there, have led critics to term him "The Incurable Rebel." 14.____
    B. The President's program was not always received with the wholehearted endorsement of his own party, which is why the party faces difficulty in drawing up a platform for the coming election.
    C. The reason why they wanted to travel was because they had never been away from home.
    D. Facing a barrage of cameras, the visiting celebrity found it extremely difficult to express his opinions clearly.

15. A. When we calmed down, we all agreed that our anger had been kind of unnecessary and had not helped the situation. 15.____
    B. Without him going into all the details, he made us realize the horror of the accident.
    C. Like one girl, for example, who applied for two positions.
    D. Do not think that you have to be so talented as he is in order to play in the school orchestra.

16. A. He looked very peculiarly to me. 16.____
    B. He certainly looked at me peculiar.
    C. Due to the train's being late, we had to wait an hour.
    D. The reason for the poor attendance is that it is raining.

17. A. About one out of four own an automobile. 17.____
    B. The collapse of the old Mitchell Bridge was caused by defective construction in the central pier.
    C. Brooks Atkinson was well acquainted with the best literature, thus helping him to become an able critic.
    D. He has to stand still until the relief man comes up, thus giving him no chance to move about and keep warm.

18. A. He is sensitive to confusion and withdraws from people whom he feels are too noisy. 18.____
    B. Do you know whether the data is statistically correct?
    C. Neither the mayor or the aldermen are to blame.
    D. Of those who were graduated from high school, a goodly percentage went to college.

19. A. Acting on orders, the offices were searched by a designated committee. 19.____
    B. The answer probably is nothing.
    C. I thought it to be all right to excuse them from class.
    D. I think that he is as successful a singer, if not more successful, than Mary.

20. A. $120,000 is really very little to pay for such a wellbuilt house.
    B. The creatures looked like they had come from outer space.
    C. It was her, he knew!
    D. Nobody but me knows what to do.

21. A. Mrs. Smith looked good in her new suit.
    B. New York may be compared with Chicago.
    C. I will not go to the meeting except you go with me.
    D. I agree with this editorial.

22. A. My opinions are different from his.
    B. There will be less students in class now.
    C. Helen was real glad to find her watch.
    D. It had been pushed off of her dresser.

23. A. Almost everone, who has been to California, returns with glowing reports.
    B. George Washington, John Adams, and Thomas Jefferson, were our first presidents.
    C. Mr. Walters, whom we met at the bank yesterday, is the man, who gave me my first job.
    D. One should study his lessons as carefully as he can.

24. A. We had such a good time yesterday.
    B. When the bell rang, the boys and girls went in the schoolhouse.
    C. John had the worst headache when he got up this morning.
    D. Today's assignment is somewhat longer than yesterday's.

25. A. Neither the mayor nor the city clerk are willing to talk.
    B. Neither the mayor nor the city clerk is willing to talk.
    C. Neither the mayor or the city clerk are willing to talk.
    D. Neither the mayor or the city clerk is willing to talk.

26. A. Being that he is that kind of boy, cooperation cannot be expected.
    B. He interviewed people who he thought had something to say.
    C. Stop whomever enters the building regardless of rank or office held.
    D. Passing through the countryside, the scenery pleased us.

27. A. The childrens' shoes were in their closet.
    B. The children's shoes were in their closet.
    C. The childs' shoes were in their closet.
    D. The childs' shoes were in his closet.

28. A. An agreement was reached between the defendant, the plaintiff, the plaintiff's attorney and the insurance company as to the amount of the settlement.
    B. Everybody was asked to give their versions of the accident.
    C. The consensus of opinion was that the evidence was inconclusive.
    D. The witness stated that if he was rich, he wouldn't have had to loan the money.

29.
- A. Before beginning the investigation, all the materials relating to the case were carefully assembled.
- B. The reason for his inability to keep the appointment is because of his injury in the accident.
- C. This here evidence tends to support the claim of the defendant.
- D. We interviewed all the witnesses who, according to the driver, were still in town.

29.____

30.
- A. Each claimant was allowed the full amount of their medical expenses.
- B. Either of the three witnesses is available.
- C. Every one of the witnesses was asked to tell his story.
- D. Neither of the witnesses are right.

30.____

31.
- A. The commissioner, as well as his deputy and various bureau heads, were present.
- B. A new organization of employers and employees have been formed.
- C. One or the other of these men have been selected.
- D. The number of pages in the book is enough to discourage a reader.

31.____

32.
- A. Between you and me, I think he is the better man.
- B. He was believed to be me.
- C. Is it us that you wish to see?
- D. The winners are him and her.

32.____

33.
- A. Beside the statement to the police, the witness spoke to no one.
- B. He made no statement other than to the police and I.
- C. He made no statement to any one else, aside from the police.
- D. The witness spoke to no one but me.

33.____

34.
- A. The claimant has no one to blame but himself.
- B. The boss sent us, he and I, to deliver the packages.
- C. The lights come from mine and not his car.
- D. There was room on the stairs for him and myself.

34.____

35.
- A. Admission to this clinic is limited to patients' inability to pay for medical care.
- B. Patients who can pay little or nothing for medical care are treated in this clinic.
- C. The patient's ability to pay for medical care is the determining factor in his admissibility to this clinic.
- D. This clinic is for the patient's that cannot afford to pay or that can pay a little for medical care.

35.____

KEY (CORRECT ANSWERS)

1.	A		16.	D
2.	A		17.	B
3.	D		18.	D
4.	C		19.	B
5.	D		20.	D
6.	D		21.	A
7.	B		22.	A
8.	B		23.	D
9.	D		24.	D
10.	B		25.	B
11.	C		26.	B
12.	B		27.	B
13.	D		28.	C
14.	D		29.	D
15.	D		30.	C

31. D
32. A
33. D
34. A
35. B

EXAMINATION SECTION
TEST 1

DIRECTIONS: Each question or incomplete statement is followed by several suggested answers or completions. Select the one that BEST answers the question or completes the statement. *PRINT THE LETTER OF THE CORRECT ANSWER IN THE SPACE AT THE RIGHT.*

1. Which of the following sentences is punctuated INCORRECTLY? 1.____

    A. Johnson said, "One tiny virus, Blanche, can multiply so fast that it will become 200 viruses in 25 minutes."
    B. With economic pressures hitting them from all sides, American farmers have become the weak link in the food chain.
    C. The degree to which this is true, of course, depends on the personalities of the people involved, the subject matter, and the atmosphere in general.
    D. "What loneliness, asked George Eliot, is more lonely than distrust?"

2. Which of the following sentences is punctuated INCORRECTLY? 2.____

    A. Based on past experiences, do you expect the plumber to show up late, not have the right parts, and overcharge you.
    B. When polled, however, the participants were most concerned that it be convenient.
    C. No one mentioned the flavor of the coffee, and no one seemed to care that china was used instead of plastic.
    D. As we said before, sometimes people view others as things; they don't see them as living, breathing beings like themselves.

3. Convention members travelled here from Kingston New York Pittsfield Massachusetts Bennington Vermont and Hartford Connecticut. 3.____
   How many commas should there be in the above sentence?

    A. 3 B. 4 C. 5 D. 6

4. Of the two speakers the one who spoke about human rights is more famous and more humble. 4.____
   How many commas should there be in the above sentence?

    A. 1 B. 2 C. 3 D. 4

5. Which sentence is punctuated INCORRECTLY? 5.____

    A. Five people voted no; two voted yes; one person abstained.
    B. Well, consider what has been said here today, but we won't make any promises.
    C. Anthropologists divide history into three major periods: the Stone Age, the Bronze Age, and the Iron Age.
    D. Therefore, we may create a stereotype about people who are unsuccessful; we may see them as lazy, unintelligent, or afraid of success.

6. Which sentence is punctuated INCORRECTLY? 6.____

    A. Studies have found that the unpredictability of customer behavior can lead to a great deal of stress, particularly if the behavior is unpleasant or if the employee has little control over it.

B. If this degree of emotion and variation can occur in spectator sports, imagine the role that perceptions can play when there are real stakes involved.
C. At other times, however hidden expectations may sabotage or severely damage an encounter without anyone knowing what happened.
D. There are usually four issues to look for in a conflict: differences in values, goals, methods, and facts.

Questions 7-10.

DIRECTIONS: Questions 7 through 10 test your ability to distinguish between words that sound alike but are spelled differently and have different meanings. In the following groups of sentences, one of the underlined words is used incorrectly.

7. A. By accepting responsibility for their actions, managers promote trust.
   B. Dropping hints or making illusions to things that you would like changed sometimes leads to resentment.
   C. The entire unit loses respect for the manager and resents the reprimand.
   D. Many people are averse to confronting problems directly; they would rather avoid them.

7.____

8. A. What does this say about the effect our expectations have on those we supervise?
   B. In an effort to save time between 9 A.M. and 1 P.M., the staff members devised their own interpretation of what was to be done on these forms.
   C. The task master's principal concern is for getting the work done; he or she is not concerned about the needs or interests of employees.
   D. The advisor's main objective was increasing Angela's ability to invest her capitol wisely.

8.____

9. A. A typical problem is that people have to cope with the internal censer of their feelings.
   B. Sometimes, in their attempt to sound more learned, people speak in ways that are barely comprehensible.
   C. The council will meet next Friday to decide whether Abrams should continue as representative.
   D. His descent from grace was assured by that final word.

9.____

10. A. The doctor said that John's leg had to remain stationary or it would not heal properly.
    B. There is a city ordinance against parking too close to fire hydrants.
    C. Meyer's problem is that he is never discrete when talking about office politics.
    D. Mrs. Thatcher probably worked harder than any other British Prime Minister had ever worked.

10.____

Questions 11-20.

DIRECTIONS: For each of the following groups of sentences in Questions 11 through 20, select the sentence which is the BEST example of English usage and grammar.

11. A. She is a woman who, at age sixty, is distinctly attractive and cares about how they look.
    B. It was a seemingly impossible search, and no one knew the problems better than she.
    C. On the surface, they are all sweetness and light, but his morbid character is under it.
    D. The minicopier, designed to appeal to those who do business on the run like architects in the field or business travelers, weigh about four pounds.

11.____

12. A. Neither the administrators nor the union representative regret the decision to settle the disagreement.
    B. The plans which are made earlier this year were no longer being considered.
    C. I would have rode with him if I had known he was leaving at five.
    D. I don't know who she said had it.

12.____

13. A. Writing at a desk, the memo was handed to her for immediate attention.
    B. Carla didn't water Carl's plants this week, which she never does.
    C. Not only are they good workers, with excellent writing and speaking skills, and they get to the crux of any problem we hand them.
    D. We've noticed that this enthusiasm for undertaking new projects sometimes interferes with his attention to detail.

13.____

14. A. It's obvious that Nick offends people by being unruly, inattentive, and having no patience.
    B. Marcia told Genie that she would have to leave soon.
    C. Here are the papers you need to complete your investigation.
    D. Julio was startled by you're comment.

14.____

15. A. The new manager has done good since receiving her promotion, but her secretary has helped her a great deal.
    B. One of the personnel managers approached John and tells him that the client arrived unexpectedly.
    C. If somebody can supply us with the correct figures, they should do so immediately.
    D. Like zealots, advocates seek power because they want to influence the policies and actions of an organization.

15.____

16. A. Between you and me, Chris probably won't finish this assignment in time.
    B. Rounding the corner, the snack bar appeared before us.
    C. Parker's radical reputation made to the Supreme Court his appointment impossible.
    D. By the time we arrived, Marion finishes briefing James and returns to Hank's office.

16.____

17. A. As we pointed out earlier, the critical determinant of the success of middle managers is their ability to communicate well with others.
    B. The lecturer stated there wasn't no reason for bad supervision.
    C. We are well aware whose at fault in this instance.
    D. When planning important changes, it's often wise to seek the participation of others because employees often have much valuable ideas to offer.

17.____

18. A. Joan had ought to throw out those old things that were damaged when the roof leaked.
    B. I spose he'll let us know what he's decided when he finally comes to a decision.
    C. Carmen was walking to work when she suddenly realized that she had left her lunch on the table as she passed the market.
    D. Are these enough plants for your new office?

18.____

19. A. First move the lever forward, and then they should lift the ribbon casing before trying to take it out.
    B. Michael finished quickest than any other person in the office.
    C. There is a special meeting for we committee members today at 4 p.m.
    D. My husband is worried about our having to work overtime next week.

19.____

20. A. Another source of conflicts are individuals who possess very poor interpersonal skills.
    B. It is difficult for us to work with him on projects because these kinds of people are not interested in team building.
    C. Each of the departments was represented at the meeting.
    D. Poor boy, he never should of past that truck on the right.

20.____

Questions 21-28.

DIRECTIONS: In Questions 21 through 28, there may be a problem with English grammar or usage. If a problem does exist, select the letter that indicates the most effective change. If no problem exists, select choice A.

21. He rushed her to the hospital and stayed with her, even though this took quite a bit of his time, he didn't charge her anything.

21.____

    A. No changes are necessary
    B. Change even though to although
    C. Change the first comma to a period and capitalize even
    D. Change rushed to had rushed

22. Waiting that appears unfairly feels longer than waiting that seems justified.

22.____

    A. No changes are necessary
    B. Change unfairly to unfair
    C. Change appears to seems
    D. Change longer to longest

4 (#1)

86

23. May be you and the person who argued with you will be able to reach an agreement. 23.____

    A. No changes are necessary
    B. Change will be to were
    C. Change argued with to had an argument with
    D. Change May be to Maybe

24. Any one of them could of taken the file while you were having coffee. 24.____

    A. No changes are necessary
    B. Change any one to anyone
    C. Change of to have
    D. Change were having to were out having

25. While people get jobs or move from poverty level to better paying employment, they stop receiving benefits and start paying taxes. 25.____

    A. No changes are necessary
    B. Change While to As
    C. Change stop to will stop
    D. Change get to obtain

26. Maribeth's phone rang while talking to George about the possibility of their meeting Tom at three this afternoon. 26.____

    A. No changes are necessary
    B. Change their to her
    C. Move to George so that it follows Tom
    D. Change talking to she was talking

27. According to their father, Lisa is smarter than Chris, but Emily is the smartest of the three sisters. 27.____

    A. No changes are necessary
    B. Change their to her
    C. Change is to was
    D. Make two sentences, changing the second comma to a period and omitting but

28. Yesterday, Mark and he claim that Carl took Carol's ideas and used them inappropriately. 28.____

    A. No changes are necessary
    B. Change claim to claimed
    C. Change inappropriately to inappropriate
    D. Change Carol's to Carols'

Questions 29-34.

DIRECTIONS: For each group of sentences in Questions 29 through 34, select the choice that represents the BEST editing of the problem sentence.

29. The managers expected employees to be at their desks at all times, but they would always be late or leave unannounced. 29.____

A. The managers wanted employees to always be at their desks, but they would always be late or leave unannounced.
B. Although the managers expected employees to be at their desks no matter what came up, they would always be late and leave without telling anyone.
C. Although the managers expected employees to be at their desks at all times, the managers would always be late or leave without telling anyone.
D. The managers expected the employee to never leave their desks, but they would always be late or leave without telling anyone.

30. The one who is department manager he will call you to discuss the problem tomorrow morning at 10 A.M. 30.____

    A. The one who is department manager will call you tomorrow morning at ten to discuss the problem.
    B. The department manager will call you to discuss the problem tomorrow at 10 A.M.
    C. Tomorrow morning at 10 A.M., the department manager will call you to discuss the problem.
    D. Tomorrow morning the department manager will call you to discuss the problem.

31. A conference on child care in the workplace the $200 cost of which to attend may be prohibitive to childcare workers who earn less than that weekly. 31.____

    A. A conference on child care in the workplace that costs $200 may be too expensive for childcare workers who earn less than that each week.
    B. A conference on child care in the workplace, the cost of which to attend is $200, may be prohibitive to childcare workers who earn less than that weekly.
    C. A conference on child care in the workplace who costs $200 may be too expensive for childcare workers who earn less than that a week.
    D. A conference on child care in the workplace which costs $200 may be too expensive to childcare workers who earn less than that on a weekly basis.

32. In accordance with estimates recently made, there are 40,000 to 50,000 nuclear weapons in our world today. 32.____

    A. Because of estimates recently, there are 40,000 to 50,000 nuclear weapons in the world today.
    B. In accordance with estimates made recently, there are 40,000 to 50,000 nuclear weapons in the world today.
    C. According to estimates made recently, there are 40,000 to 50,000 weapons in the world today.
    D. According to recent estimates, there are 40,000 to 50,000 nuclear weapons in the world today.

33. Motivation is important in problem solving, but they say that excessive motivation can inhibit the creative process. 33.____

    A. Motivation is important in problem solving, but, as they say, too much of it can inhibit the creative process.
    B. Motivation is important in problem solving and excessive motivation will inhibit the creative process.
    C. Motivation is important in problem solving, but excessive motivation can inhibit the creative process.

D. Motivation is important in problem solving because excessive motivation can inhibit the creative process.

34. In selecting the best option calls for consulting with all the people that are involved in it. 34._____

   A. In selecting the best option consulting with all the people concerned with it.
   B. Calling for the best option, we consulted all the affected people.
   C. We called all the people involved to select the best option.
   D. To be sure of selecting the best option, one should consult all the people involved.

35. There are a number of problems with the following letter. From the options below, select the version that is MOST in accordance with standard business style, tone, and form. 35._____

Dear Sir:

We are so sorry that we have had to backorder your order for 15,000 widgets and 2,300 whatzits for such a long time. We have been having incredibly bad luck lately. When your order first came in no one could get to it because my secretary was out with the flu and her replacement didn't know what she was doing, then there was the dock strike in Cucamonga which held things up for awhile, and then it just somehow got lost. We think it may have fallen behind the radiator.

We are happy to say that all these problems have been taken care of, we are caught up on supplies, and we should have the stuff to you soon, in the near future --about two weeks. You may not believe us after everything you've been through with us, but it's true.

We'll let you know as soon as we have a secure date for delivery. Thank you so much for continuing to do business with us after all the problems this probably has caused you.

Yours very sincerely,

Rob Barker

   A. Dear Sir:

   We are so sorry that we have had to backorder your order for 15,000 widgets and 2,300 whatzits. We have been having problems with staff lately and the dock strike hasn't helped anything.

   We are happy to say that all these problems have been taken care of. I've told my secretary to get right on it, and we should have the stuff to you soon. Thank you so much for continuing to do business with us after all the problems this must have caused you.

   We'll let you know as soon as we have a secure date for delivery.

   Sincerely,

   Rob Barker

B. Dear Sir:

We regret that we haven't been able to fill your order for 15,000 widgets and 2,300 whatzits in a timely fashion.

We'll let you know as soon as we have a secure date for delivery.

Sincerely,

Rob Barker

C. Dear Sir:

We are so very sorry that we haven't been able to fill your order for 15,000 widgets and 2,300 whatzits. We have been having incredibly bad luck lately, but things are much better now.

Thank you so much for bearing with us through all of this. We'll let you know as soon as we have a secure date for delivery.

Sincerely,

Rob Barker

D. Dear Sir:

We are very sorry that we haven't been able to fill your order for 15,000 widgets and 2,300 whatzits. Due to unforeseen difficulties, we have had to back-order your request. At this time, supplies have caught up to demand, and we foresee a delivery date within the next two weeks.

We'll let you know as soon as we have a secure date for delivery. Thank you for your patience.

Sincerely,

Rob Barker

KEY (CORRECT ANSWERS)

1.	D	16.	A
2.	A	17.	A
3.	B	18.	D
4.	A	19.	D
5.	B	20.	C
6.	C	21.	C
7.	B	22.	B
8.	D	23.	D
9.	A	24.	C
10.	C	25.	B
11.	B	26.	D
12.	D	27.	A
13.	D	28.	B
14.	C	29.	C
15.	D	30.	B

31.	A
32.	D
33.	C
34.	D
35.	D

EXAMINATION SECTION
TEST 1

DIRECTIONS: In each of the following tests in this part, select the letter of the one MIS-SPELLED word in each of the following groups of words. If no word is misspelled, select the last item, letter E (none misspelled). *PRINT THE LETTER OF THE CORRECT ANSWER IN THE SPACE AT THE RIGHT.*

1. A. grateful B. fundimental C. census 1.____
   D. analysis E. NONE MISSPELLED

2. A. installment B. retrieve C. concede 2.____
   D. dissapear E. NONE MISSPELLED

3. A. accidentaly B. dismissal C. conscientious 3.____
   D. indelible E. NONE MISSPELLED

4. A. perceive B. carreer C. anticipate 4.____
   D. acquire E. NONE MISSPELLED

5. A. facility B. reimburse C. assortment 5.____
   D. guidance E. NONE MISSPELLED

6. A. plentiful B. across C. advantagous 6.____
   D. similar E. NONE MISSPELLED

7. A. omission B. pamphlet C. guarrantee 7.____
   D. repel E. NONE MISSPELLED

8. A. maintenance B. always C. liable 8.____
   D. anouncement E. NONE MISSPELLED

9. A. exaggerate B. sieze C. condemn 9.____
   D. commit E. NONE MISSPELLED

10. A. pospone B. altogether C. grievance 10.____
    D. excessive E. NONE MISSPELLED

11. A. arguing B. correspondance C. forfeit 11.____
    D. dissension E. NONE MISSPELLED

12. A. occasion B. description C. prejudice 12.____
    D. elegible E. NONE MISSPELLED

13. A. accomodate B. initiative C. changeable 13.____
    D. enroll E. NONE MISSPELLED

14. A. temporary B. insistent C. benificial 14.____
    D. separate E. NONE MISSPELLED

15. A. achieve B. dissapoint C. unanimous 15.____
    D. judgment E. NONE MISSPELLED

16. A. proceed B. publicly C. sincerity 16.____
    D. successful E. NONE MISSPELLED

17.	A.	deceive	B.	goverment	C.	preferable		17._____
	D.	repetitive	E.	*NONE MISSPELLED*				
18.	A.	emphasis	B.	skillful	C.	advisible		18._____
	D.	optimistic	E.	*NONE MISSPELLED*				
19.	A.	tendency	B.	rescind	C.	crucial		19._____
	D.	noticable	E.	*NONE MISSPELLED*				
20.	A.	privelege	B.	abbreviate	C.	simplify		20._____
	D.	divisible	E.	*NONE MISSPELLED*				

KEY (CORRECT ANSWERS)

1. B. fundamental
2. D. disappear
3. A. accidentally
4. B. career
5. E. None Misspelled
6. C. advantageous
7. C. guarantee
8. D. announcement
9. B. seize
10. A. postpone
11. B. correspondence
12. D. eligible
13. A. accommodate
14. C. beneficial
15. B. disappoint
16. E. None Misspelled
17. B. government
18. C. advisable
19. D. noticeable
20. A. privilege

TEST 2

DIRECTIONS: In each of the following tests in this part, select the letter of the one MIS-SPELLED word in each of the following groups of words. If no word is misspelled, select the last item, letter E (none misspelled). *PRINT THE LETTER OF THE CORRECT ANSWER IN THE SPACE AT THE RIGHT.*

1. A. typical B. descend C. summarize D. continuel E. NONE MISSPELLED 1.____

2. A. courageous B. recomend C. omission D. eliminate E. NONE MISSPELLED 2.____

3. A. compliment B. illuminate C. auxilary D. installation E. NONE MISSPELLED 3.____

4. A. preliminary B. aquainted C. syllable D. analysis E. NONE MISSPELLED 4.____

5. A. accustomed B. negligible C. interupted D. bulletin E. NONE MISSPELLED 5.____

6. A. summoned B. managment C. mechanism D. sequence E. NONE MISSPELLED 6.____

7. A. commitee B. surprise C. noticeable D. emphasize E. NONE MISSPELLED 7.____

8. A. occurrance B. likely C. accumulate D. grievance E. grievance 8.____

9. A. obstacle B. particuliar C. baggage D. fascinating E. NONE MISSPELLED 9.____

10. A. innumerable B. seize C. applicant D. dicionery E. NONE MISSPELLED 10.____

11. A. primary B. mechanic C. referred D. admissible E. NONE MISSPELLED 11.____

12. A. cessation B. beleif C. aggressive D. allowance E. NONE MISSPELLED 12.____

13. A. leisure B. authentic C. familiar D. contemptable E. NONE MISSPELLED 13.____

14. A. volume B. forty C. dilemma D. seldum E. NONE MISSPELLED 14.____

15. A. discrepancy B. aquisition C. exorbitant D. lenient E. NONE MISSPELLED 15.____

16. A. simultanous B. penetrate C. revision D. conspicuous E. NONE MISSPELLED 16.____

17. A. ilegible B. gracious C. profitable D. obedience E. NONE MISSPELLED 17.____

95

2 (#2)

18. A. manufacturer   B. authorize   C. compelling   18.____
    D. pecular   E. *NONE MISSPELLED*

19. A. anxious   B. rehearsal   C. handicaped   19.____
    D. tendency   E. *NONE MISSPELLED*

20. A. meticulous   B. accompaning   C. initiative   20.____
    D. shelves   E. *NONE MISSPELLED*

KEY (CORRECT ANSWERS)

1. D. continual
2. B. recommend
3. C. auxiliary
4. B. acquainted
5. C. interrupted
6. B. management
7. A. committee
8. A. occurrence
9. B. particular
10. D. dictionary
11. E. None Misspelled
12. B. belief
13. D. contemptible
14. D. seldom
15. B. acquisition
16. A. simultaneous
17. A. illegible
18. D. peculiar
19. C. handicapped
20. B. accompanying

TEST 3

DIRECTIONS: In each of the following tests in this part, select the letter of the one MIS-SPELLED word in each of the following groups of words. If no word is misspelled, select the last item, letter E (none misspelled). *PRINT THE LETTER OF THE CORRECT ANSWER IN THE SPACE AT THE RIGHT.*

1. A. grievous B. dilettante C. gibberish 1.____
   D. upbraid E. NONE MISSPELLED

2. A. embarrassing B. playright C. unmanageable 2.____
   D. symmetrical E. NONE MISSPELLED

3. A. sestet B. denouement C. liaison 3.____
   D. tattooing E. NONE MISSPELLED

4. A. prophesied B. soliliquy C. supersede 4.____
   D. hemorrhage E. NONE MISSPELLED

5. A. colossal B. renascent C. parallel 5.____
   D. omnivorous E. NONE MISSPELLED

6. A. passable B. dispensable C. deductable 6.____
   D. irreducible E. NONE MISSPELLED

7. A. guerrila B. carousal C. maneuver 7.____
   D. staid E. NONE MISSPELLED

8. A. maintenance B. mountainous C. sustenance 8.____
   D. gluttinous E. NONE MISSPELLED

9. A. holocaust B. irascible C. buccanneer 9.____
   D. mischievous E. NONE MISSPELLED

10. A. diphthong B. rhododendron C. inviegle 10.____
    D. shellacked E. NONE MISSPELLED

11. A. Phillipines B. currant C. dietitian 11.____
    D. coercion E. NONE MISSPELLED

12. A. courtesey B. buoyancy C. fiery 12.____
    D. shepherd E. NONE MISSPELLED

13. A. censor B. queue C. obbligato 13.____
    D. antartic E. NONE MISSPELLED

14. A. chrystal B. chrysanthemum C. chrysalis 14.____
    D. chrome E. NONE MISSPELLED

15. A. shreik B. siege C. sheik 15.____
    D. sieve E. NONE MISSPELLED

16. A. leisure B. gladioluses C. kindergarden 16.____
    D. tonnage E. NONE MISSPELLED

17. A. emminent B. imminent C. blatant 17.____
    D. privilege E. NONE MISSPELLED

18. A. diphtheria   B. collander   C. seize   18.____
    D. sleight   E. *NONE MISSPELLED*

19. A. frolicking   B. caramel   C. germaine   19.____
    D. kohlrabi   E. *NONE MISSPELLED*

20. A. dispensable   B. compatable   C. recommend   20.____
    D. feasible   E. *NONE MISSPELLED*

KEY (CORRECT ANSWERS)

1. E. None Misspelled
2. B. playwright
3. E. None Misspelled
4. B. soliloquy
5. E. None Misspelled
6. C. deductible
7. A. guerrilla
8. D. gluttonous
9. C. buccaneer
10. C. inveigle
11. A. Philippines
12. A. courtesy
13. D. antarctic
14. A. crystal
15. A. shriek
16. C. kindergarten
17. A. eminent
18. B. colander
19. C. germane
20. B. compatible

TEST 4

DIRECTIONS: In each of the following tests in this part, select the letter of the one MIS-SPELLED word in each of the following groups of words. If no word is misspelled, select the last item, letter E (none misspelled). *PRINT THE LETTER OF THE CORRECT ANSWER IN THE SPACE AT THE RIGHT.*

1. A. coercion   B. rescission   C. license   1.____
   D. prophecied   E. NONE MISSPELLED

2. A. calcimine   B. seive   C. procedure   2.____
   D. poinsettia   E. NONE MISSPELLED

3. A. entymology   B. echoing   C. subtly   3.____
   D. stupefy   E. NONE MISSPELLED

4. A. mocassin   B. assassin   C. battalion   4.____
   D. despicable   E. NONE MISSPELLED

5. A. moustache   B. sovereignty   C. drunkeness   5.____
   D. staccato   E. NONE MISSPELLED

6. A. notoriety   B. stereotype   C. trellis   6.____
   D. Uraguay   E. NONE MISSPELLED

7. A. hummock   B. idiosyncrasy   C. licentiate   7.____
   D. plagiarism   E. NONE MISSPELLED

8. A. denim   B. hyssop   C. innoculate   8.____
   D. malevolent   E. NONE MISSPELLED

9. A. boundaries   B. corpulency   C. gauge   9.____
   D. jingoes   E. NONE MISSPELLED

10. A. assassin   B. refulgeant   C. sorghum   10.____
    D. suture   E. NONE MISSPELLED

11. A. dormatory   B. glimpse   C. mediocre   11.____
    D. repetition   E. NONE MISSPELLED

12. A. ambergris   B. docility   C. loquacious   12.____
    D. Pharoah   E. NONE MISSPELLED

13. A. curriculum   B. ninety-eighth   C. occurrence   13.____
    D. repertoire   E. NONE MISSPELLED

14. A. belladonna   B. equable   C. immersion   14.____
    D. naphtha   E. NONE MISSPELLED

15. A. itinerary   B. ptomaine   C. similar   15.____
    D. solicetous   E. NONE MISSPELLED

16. A. liquify   B. mausoleum   C. Philippines   16.____
    D. singeing   E. NONE MISSPELLED

17. A. descendant   B. harrassed   C. implausible   17.____
    D. irreverence   E. NONE MISSPELLED

99

2 (#4)

18. A. crystallize B. imperceptible C. isinglass 18.____
    D. precede   E. *NONE MISSPELLED*

19. A. accommodate B. deferential C. gazeteer 19.____
    D. plenteous   E. *NONE MISSPELLED*

20. A. aching   B. buttress   C. indigenous 20.____
    D. mischievous E. *NONE MISSPELLED*

KEY (CORRECT ANSWERS)

1. D. prophesied
2. B. sieve
3. A. entomology
4. A. moccasin
5. C. drunkenness
6. D. Uruguay
7. E. None Misspelled
8. C. inoculate
9. E. None Misspelled
10. B. refulgent
11. A. dormitory
12. D. Pharaoh
13. E. None Misspelled
14. E. None misspelled
15. D. solicitous
16. A. liquefy
17. B. harassed
18. E. None Misspelled
19. C. gazetteer
20. E. None Misspelled

TEST 5

DIRECTIONS: In each of the following tests in this part, select the letter of the one MIS-SPELLED word in each of the following groups of words. If no word is misspelled, select the last item, letter E (none misspelled). *PRINT THE LETTER OF THE CORRECT ANSWER IN THE SPACE AT THE RIGHT.*

1. A. comensurable B. fracas C. obeisance 1._____
    D. remittent E. NONE MISSPELLED

2. A. defiance B. delapidated C. motley 2._____
    D. rueful E. NONE MISSPELLED

3. A. demeanor B. epoch C. furtive 3._____
    D. parley E. NONE MISSPELLED

4. A. disciples B. influencial C. nemesis 4._____
    D. poultry E. NONE MISSPELLED

5. A. decision B. encourage C. incidental 5._____
    D. satyr E. NONE MISSPELLED

6. A. collate B. connivance C. luxurient 6._____
    D. manageable E. NONE MISSPELLED

7. A. constituencies B. crocheted C. foreclosure 7._____
    D. scintillating E. NONE MISSPELLED

8. A. arraignment B. assassination C. carburator 8._____
    D. irrationally E. NONE MISSPELLED

9. A. livelihood B. noticeable C. optomiatic 9._____
    D. psychology E. NONE MISSPELLED

10. A. daub B. massacre C. repitition 10._____
    D. requiem E. NONE MISSPELLED

11. A. adversary B. beneficiary C. cemetery 11._____
    D. desultory E. NONE MISSPELLED

12. A. criterion B. elicit C. incredulity 12._____
    D. omnishient E. NONE MISSPELLED

13. A. dining B. fiery C. incidentally 13._____
    D. rheumatism E. NONE MISSPELLED

14. A. collaborator B. gaudey C. habilitation 14._____
    D. logician E. NONE MISSPELLED

15. A. dirge B. ogle C. recumbent 15._____
    D. reminiscence E. NONE MISSPELLED

16. A. conscientious B. renunciation C. inconvenient 16._____
    D. inoculate E. NONE MISSPELLED

17. A. crystalline B. scimitar C. ecstacy 17._____
    D. vestigial E. NONE MISSPELLED

101

18. A. phlegmatic B. rhythm C. plebescite 18.____
    D. refectory E. *NONE MISSPELLED*

19. A. resilient B. resevoir C. recipient 19.____
    D. sobriety E. *NONE MISSPELLED*

20. A. privilege B. leige C. leisure 20.____
    D. basilisk E. *NONE MISSPELLED*

KEY (CORRECT ANSWERS)

1. A. commensurable
2. B. dilapidated
3. E. None Misspelled
4. B. influential
5. E. None Misspelled
6. C. luxuriant
7. E. None Misspelled
8. C. carburetor
9. C. optimistic
10. C. repetition
11. E. None Misspelled
12. D. omniscient
13. E. None Misspelled
14. B. gaudy
15. E. None Misspelled
16. E. None Misspelled
17. C. ecstasy
18. C. plebiscite
19. B. reservoir
20. B. liege

TEST 6

DIRECTIONS: In each of the following tests in this part, select the letter of the one MIS-SPELLED word in each of the following groups of words. If no word is misspelled, select the last item, letter E (none misspelled). *PRINT THE LETTER OF THE CORRECT ANSWER IN THE SPACE AT THE RIGHT.*

1. A. repellent B. elliptical C. paralelling D. colossal E. NONE MISSPELLED 1.____

2. A. uproarious B. grievous C. armature D. tabular E. NONE MISSPELLED 2.____

3. A. ammassed B. embarrassed C. promissory D. asymmetrical E. NONE MISSPELLED 3.____

4. A. maintenance B. correspondence C. benificence D. miasmic E. NONE MISSPELLED 4.____

5. A. demurred B. occurrence C. temperament D. abhorrance E. NONE MISSPELLED 5.____

6. A. proboscis B. lucious C. mischievous D. vilify E. NONE MISSPELLED 6.____

7. A. feasable B. divisible C. permeable D. forcible E. NONE MISSPELLED 7.____

8. A. courteous B. venemous C. heterogeneous D. lustrous E. NONE MISSPELLED 8.____

9. A. millionaire B. mayonnaise C. questionaire D. silhouette E. NONE MISSPELLED 9.____

10. A. contemptible B. irreverent C. illimitable D. inveigled E. NONE MISSPELLED 10.____

11. A. prevalent B. irrelavent C. ecstasy D. auxiliary E. NONE MISSPELLED 11.____

12. A. impeccable B. raillery C. precede D. occurrence E. NONE MISSPELLED 12.____

13. A. patrolling B. vignette C. ninety D. surveilance E. NONE MISSPELLED 13.____

14. A. holocaust B. incidently C. weird D. canceled E. NONE MISSPELLED 14.____

15. A. emmendation B. gratuitous C. fissionable D. dilemma E. NONE MISSPELLED 15.____

16. A. harass B. innuendo C. capilary D. pachyderm E. NONE MISSPELLED 16.____

17. A. concomitant B. Lilliputian C. sarcophagus D. melifluous E. NONE MISSPELLED 17.____

2(#6)

18. A. interpolate   B. disident   C. venal   18.____
    D. inveigh   E. *NONE MISSPELLED*

19. A. supercillious B. biennial   C. gargantuan   19.____
    D. irresistible E. *NONE MISSPELLED*

20. A. conniving   B. expedite   C. inflammible   20.____
    D. incorruptible E. *NONE MISSPELLED*

KEY (CORRECT ANSWERS)

1. C. paralleling
2. E. None Misspelled
3. A. amassed
4. C. beneficence
5. D. abhorrence
6. B. luscious
7. A. feasible
8. B. venomous
9. C. questionnaire
10. E. None Misspelled
11. B. irrelevant
12. E. None Misspelled
13. D. surveillance
14. B. incidentally
15. A. emendation
16. C. capillary
17. D. mellifluous
18. B. dissident
19. A. supercilious
20. C. inflammable

TEST 7

DIRECTIONS: In each of the following tests in this part, select the letter of the one MIS-SPELLED word in each of the following groups of words. If no word is misspelled, select the last item, letter E (none misspelled). *PRINT THE LETTER OF THE CORRECT ANSWER IN THE SPACE AT THE RIGHT.*

1. A. torturous B. omniscient C. hymenial 1.____
   D. flaccid E. *NONE MISSPELLED*

2. A. seige B. seize C. frieze 2.____
   D. grieve E. *NONE MISSPELLED*

3. A. indispensible B. euphony C. victuals 3.____
   D. receptacle E. *NONE MISSPELLED*

4. A. schism B. fortissimo C. innocuous 4.____
   D. epicurian E. *NONE MISSPELLED*

5. A. sustenance B. vilefy C. maintenance 5.____
   D. rarefy E. *NONE MISSPELLED*

6. A. desiccated B. alleviate C. beneficence 6.____
   D. preponderance E. *NONE MISSPELLED*

7. A. battalion B. incubus C. sacrilegious 7.____
   D. innert E. *NONE MISSPELLED*

8. A. shiboleth B. connoisseur C. potpourri 8.____
   D. dichotomy E. *NONE MISSPELLED*

9. A. pamphlet B. similar C. parlament 9.____
   D. benefited E. *NONE MISSPELLED*

10. A. genealogy B. tyrannical C. diletante 10.____
    D. abhorrence E. *NONE MISSPELLED*

11. A. effeminate B. concensus C. agglomeration 11.____
    D. fission E. *NONE MISSPELLED*

12. A. narcissus B. lyceum C. odissey 12.____
    D. peccadillo E. *NONE MISSPELLED*

13. A. stupefied B. psychiatry C. onerous 13.____
    D. frieze E. *NONE MISSPELLED*

14. A. intelligible B. semaphore C. pronounciation 14.____
    D. albumen E. *NONE MISSPELLED*

15. A. annihilate B. tyrannical C. occurence 15.____
    D. allergy E. *NONE MISSPELLED*

16. A. gauging B. probossis C. specimen 16.____
    D. its E. *NONE MISSPELLED*

17. A. diphthong B. connoisseur C. iresistible 17.____
    D. dilemma E. *NONE MISSPELLED*

2(#7)

18. A. affect B. baccillus C. beige 18.____
    D. seize E. *NONE MISSPELLED*

19. A. apostasy B. sustenance C. synonym 19.____
    D. epigrammatic E. *NONE MISSPELLED*

20. A. discernable B. consul C. efflorescence 20.____
    D. complement E. *NONE MISSPELLED*

KEY (CORRECT ANSWERS)

1. C. hymeneal
2. A. siege
3. A. indispensable
4. D. epicurean
5. B. vilify
6. E. None Misspelled
7. D. inert
8. A. shibboleth
9. C. parliament
10. C. dilettante
11. B. consensus
12. C. odyssey
13. E. None Misspelled
14. C. pronunciation
15. C. occurrence
16. B. proboscis
17. C. irresistible
18. B. bacillus
19. E. None Misspelled
20. A. discernible

TEST 8

DIRECTIONS: In each of the following tests in this part, select the letter of the one MISSPELLED word in each of the following groups of words. If no word is misspelled, select the last item, letter E (none misspelled). *PRINT THE LETTER OF THE CORRECT ANSWER IN THE SPACE AT THE RIGHT.*

1. A. righteous B. seafareing C. colloquial 1._____
   D. contumely E. NONE MISSPELLED

2. A. sanitarium B. vicissitude C. mischievious 2._____
   D. chlorophyll E. NONE MISSPELLED

3. A. captain B. theirs C. asceticism 3._____
   D. acquiesced E. NONE MISSPELLED

4. A. across B. her's C. democracy 4._____
   D. signature E. NONE MISSPELLED

5. A. villain B. vacillate C. imposter 5._____
   D. temperament E. NONE MISSPELLED

6. A. idyllic B. volitile C. obloquy 6._____
   D. emendation E. NONE MISSPELLED

7. A. heinous B. sattelite C. dissident 7._____
   D. ephemeral E. NONE MISSPELLED

8. A. ennoble B. shellacked C. vilify 8._____
   D. indissoluble E. NONE MISSPELLED

9. A. argueing B. intrepid C. papyrus 9._____
   D. foulard E. NONE MISSPELLED

10. A. guttural B. acknowleging C. isosceles 10._____
    D. assonance E. NONE MISSPELLED

11. A. shoeing B. exorcise C. development 11._____
    D. irreperable E. NONE MISSPELLED

12. A. counseling B. cancellation C. kidnapped 12._____
    D. repellant E. NONE MISSPELLED

13. A. disatisfy B. misstep C. usually 13._____
    D. gregarious E. NONE MISSPELLED

14. A. unparalleled B. beggar C. embarrass 14._____
    D. ecstacy E. NONE MISSPELLED

15. A. descendant B. poliomyelitis C. privilege 15._____
    D. tragedy E. NONE MISSPELLED

16. A. nullify B. siderial C. salability 16._____
    D. irrelevant E. NONE MISSPELLED

17. A. paraphenalia B. apothecaries C. occurrence 17._____
    D. plagiarize E. NONE MISSPELLED

2 (#8)

18. A. asinine B. dissonent C. opossum 18.____
    D. indispensable E. *NONE MISSPELLED*

19. A. orifice B. deferrment C. harass 19.____
    D. accommodate E. *NONE MISSPELLED*

20. A. changeable B. therefor C. incidently 20.____
    D. dissatisfy E. *NONE MISSPELLED*

KEY (CORRECT ANSWERS)

1. B. seafaring
2. C. mischievous
3. E. None Misspelled
4. B. hers
5. C. impostor
6. B. volatile
7. B. satellite
8. E. None Misspelled
9. A. arguing
10. B. acknowledging
11. D. irreparable
12. D. repellent
13. A. dissatisfy
14. D. ecstasy
15. E. None Misspelled
16. B. sidereal
17. A. paraphernalia
18. B. dissonant
19. B. deferment
20. C. incidentally

TEST 9

DIRECTIONS: In each of the following tests in this part, select the letter of the one MISSPELLED word in each of the following groups of words. If no word is misspelled, select the last item, letter E (none misspelled). *PRINT THE LETTER OF THE CORRECT ANSWER IN THE SPACE AT THE RIGHT.*

1. A. irreparably B. lovable C. comparitively 1.____
   D. audible E. NONE MISSPELLED

2. A. vilify B. efflorescence C. sarcophagus 2.____
   D. sacreligious E. NONE MISSPELLED

3. A. picnicking B. proceedure C. hypocrisy 3.____
   D. seize E. NONE MISSPELLED

4. A. discomfit B. sapient C. exascerbate 4.____
   D. sarsaparilla E. NONE MISSPELLED

5. A. valleys B. maintainance C. abridgment 5.____
   D. reticence E. NONE MISSPELLED

6. A. idylic B. beneficent C. singeing 6.____
   D. asterisk E. NONE MISSPELLED

7. A. appropos B. violoncello C. peony 7.____
   D. mucilage E. NONE MISSPELLED

8. A. caterpillar B. silhouette C. rhapsody 8.____
   D. frieze E. NONE MISSPELLED

9. A. appendicitis B. vestigeal C. colonnade 9.____
   D. tortuous E. NONE MISSPELLED

10. A. omlet B. diphtheria C. highfalutin 10.____
    D. miniature E. NONE MISSPELLED

11. A. diorama B. sustanance C. disastrous 11.____
    D. conscious E. NONE MISSPELLED

12. A. inelegible B. irreplaceable C. dissatisfied 12.____
    D. procedural E. NONE MISSPELLED

13. A. contemptible B. sacrilegious C. proffessor 13.____
    D. privilege E. NONE MISSPELLED

14. A. inoculate B. diptheria C. gladioli 14.____
    D. hypocrisy E. NONE MISSPELLED

15. A. pessimism B. ecstasy C. furlough 15.____
    D. vulnerible E. NONE MISSPELLED

16. A. supersede B. moccasin C. recondite 16.____
    D. rhythmical E. NONE MISSPELLED

17. A. Adirondack B. Phillipines C. Czechoslovakia 17.____
    D. Cincinnati E. NONE MISSPELLED

2 (#9)

18. A. weird B. impromptu C. guerrila 18.____
    D. spontaneously E. *NONE MISSPELLED*

19. A. newstand B. accidentally C. tangible 19.____
    D. reservoir E. *NONE MISSPELLED*

20. A. macaroni B. mackerel C. ukulele 20.____
    D. giutar E. *NONE MISSPELLED*

KEY (CORRECT ANSWERS)

1. C. comparatively
2. D. sacrilegious
3. B. procedure
4. C. exacerbate
5. B. maintenance
6. A. idyllic
7. A. apropos
8. E. None Misspelled
9. B. vestigial
10. A. omelet
11. B. sustenance
12. A. ineligible
13. C. professor
14. B. diphtheria
15. D. vulnerable
16. E. None Misspelled
17. B. Philippines
18. C. guerrilla
19. A. newsstand
20. D. guitar

TEST 10

DIRECTIONS: In each of the following tests in this part, select the letter of the one MIS-SPELLED word in each of the following groups of words. If no word is misspelled, select the last item, letter E (none misspelled). *PRINT THE LETTER OF THE CORRECT ANSWER IN THE SPACE AT THE RIGHT.*

1. A. rescission B. sacrament C. hypocricy 1.____
   D. salable E. *NONE MISSPELLED*

2. A. rhythm B. foreboding C. withal 2.____
   D. consciousness E. *NONE MISSPELLED*

3. A. noticeable B. drunkenness C. frolicked 3.____
   D. abcess E. *NONE MISSPELLED*

4. A. supersede B. canoeing C. exorbitant 4.____
   D. vigilance E. *NONE MISSPELLED*

5. A. idiosyncrasy B. pantomine C. isosceles 5.____
   D. wintry E. *NONE MISSPELLED*

6. A. numbskull B. indispensable C. fatiguing 6.____
   D. gluey E. *NONE MISSPELLED*

7. A. dryly B. egregious C. recommend 7.____
   D. irresistable' E. *NONE MISSPELLED*

8. A. unforgettable B. mackeral C. perseverance 8.____
   D. rococo E. *NONE MISSPELLED*

9. A. mischievous B. tyranical C. desiccate 9.____
   D. battalion E. *NONE MISSPELLED*

10. A. accede B. ninth C. abyssmal 10.____
    D. commonalty E. *NONE MISSPELLED*

11. A. resplendent B. colonnade C. harass 11.____
    D. mimicking E. *NONE MISSPELLED*

12. A. dilletante B. pusillanimous C. grievance 12.____
    D. cataclysm E. *NONE MISSPELLED*

13. A. anomaly B. connoisseur C. feasable 13.____
    D. stationery E. *NONE MISSPELLED*

14. A. ennervated B. rescission C. vacillate 14.____
    D. raucous E. *NONE MISSPELLED*

15. A. liquefy B. poniard C. truculant 15.____
    D. weird E. *NONE MISSPELLED*

16. A. existance B. lieutenant C. asinine 16.____
    D. parallelogram E. *NONE MISSPELLED*

17. A. protuberant B. nuisance C. instrumental 17.____
    D. resevoir E. *NONE MISSPELLED*

2 (#10)

18. A. sustenance B. pedigree C. supercillious 18.____
    D. clairvoyant E. *NONE MISSPELLED*

19. A. commingle B. bizarre C. gauge 19.____
    D. priviledge E. *NONE MISSPELLED*

20. A. analagous B. irresistible C. apparel 20.____
    D. hindrance E. *NONE MISSPELLED*

KEY (CORRECT ANSWERS)

1. C. hypocrisy
2. E. None Misspelled
3. D. abscess
4. E. None Misspelled
5. B. pantomime
6. A. numskull
7. D. irresistible
8. B. mackerel
9. B. tyrannical
10. C. abysmal
11. E. None Misspelled
12. A. dilettante
13. C. feasible
14. A. enervated
15. C. truculent
16. A. existence
17. D. reservoir
18. C. supercilious
19. D. privilege
20. A. analogous

TEST 11

DIRECTIONS: In each of the following tests in this part, select the letter of the one MIS-SPELLED word in each of the following groups of words. If no word is misspelled, select the last item, letter E (none misspelled). *PRINT THE LETTER OF THE CORRECT ANSWER IN THE SPACE AT THE RIGHT.*

1. A. impute B. imparshal C. immodest 1.____
   D. imminent E. *NONE MISSPELLED*

2. A. cover B. audit C. adege 2.____
   D. adder E. *NONE MISSPELLED*

3. A. promissory B. maturity C. severally 3.____
   D. accomodation E. *NONE MISSPELLED*

4. A. superintendant B. dependence C. dependents 4.____
   D. entrance E. *NONE MISSPELLED*

5. A. managable B. navigable C. passable 5.____
   D. laughable E. *NONE MISSPELLED*

6. A. tolerance B. circumference C. insurance 6.____
   D. dominance E. *NONE MISSPELLED*

7. A. diameter B. tangent C. paralell 7.____
   D. perimeter E. *NONE MISSPELLED*

8. A. providential B. personal C. accidental 8.____
   D. diagonel E. *NONE MISSPELLED*

9. A. ballast B. ballustrade C. allotment 9.____
   D. bourgeois E. *NONE MISSPELLED*

10. A. diverse B. pedantic C. mishapen 10.____
    D. transient E. *NONE MISSPELLED*

11. A. surgeon B. sturgeon C. luncheon 11.____
    D. stancheon E. *NONE MISSPELLED*

12. A. pariah B. estrang C. conceive 12.____
    D. puncilious E. *NONE MISSPELLED*

13. A. camouflage B. serviceable C. mischievious 13.____
    D. menace E. *NONE MISSPELLED*

14. A. forefeit B. halve C. hundredth 14.____
    D. illusion E. *NONE MISSPELLED*

15. A. filial B. arras C. pantomine 15.____
    D. filament E. *NONE MISSPELLED*

16. A. llama B. madrigal C. martinet 16.____
    D. laxitive E. *NONE MISSPELLED*

17. A. symtom B. serum C. antiseptic 17.____
    D. aromatic E. *NONE MISSPELLED*

18.	A. erasable	B. irascible	C. audable	18.___
	D. laudable	E. *NONE MISSPELLED*		
19.	A. heroes	B. folios	C. sopranos	19.___
	D. cargos	E. *NONE MISSPELLED*		
20.	A. latent	B. goddess	C. aisle	20.___
	D. whose	E. *NONE MISSPELLED*		

KEY (CORRECT ANSWERS)

1. B. impartial
2. C. adage
3. D. accommodation
4. A. superintendent
5. A. manageable
6. E. None Misspelled
7. C. parallel
8. D. diagonal
9. B. balustrade
10. C. misshapen
11. D. stanchion
12. B. estrange
13. C. mischievous
14. A. forfeit
15. C. pantomime
16. D. laxative
17. A. symptom
18. C. audible
19. D. cargoes
20. E. None Misspelled

TEST 12

DIRECTIONS: In each of the following tests in this part, select the letter of the one MIS-SPELLED word in each of the following groups of words. If no word is misspelled, select the last item, letter E (none misspelled). *PRINT THE LETTER OF THE CORRECT ANSWER IN THE SPACE AT THE RIGHT.*

1.	A.	coconut	B.	bustling	C.	abducter	1.____
	D.	naphtha	E.	NONE MISSPELLED			
2.	A.	seriatim	B.	quadruped	C.	diphthong	2.____
	D.	concensus	E.	NONE MISSPELLED			
3.	A.	sanction	B.	propencity	C.	parabola	3.____
	D.	despotic	E.	NONE MISSPELLED			
4.	A.	circumstantial	B.	imbroglio	C.	coalesce	4.____
	D.	ductill	E.	NONE MISSPELLED			
5.	A.	spontaneous	B.	superlitive	C.	telepathy	5.____
	D.	thesis	E.	NONE MISSPELLED			
6.	A.	adobe	B.	apellate	C.	billion	6.____
	D.	chiropody	E.	NONE MISSPELLED			
7.	A.	combatant	B.	helium	C.	esprit de corps	7.____
	D.	debillity	E.	NONE MISSPELLED			
8.	A.	iota	B.	gopher	C.	demoralize	8.____
	D.	culvert	E.	NONE MISSPELLED			
9.	A.	invideous	B.	gourmand	C.	embryo	9.____
	D.	despicable	E.	NONE MISSPELLED			
10.	A.	dispeptic	B.	dromedary	C.	dormant	10.____
	D.	duress	E.	NONE MISSPELLED			
11.	A.	spiggot	B.	suffrage	C.	technology	11.____
	D.	thermostat	E.	NONE MISSPELLED			
12.	A.	aberration	B.	antropology	C.	bayou	12.____
	D.	cashew	E.	NONE MISSPELLED			
13.	A.	ricochet	B.	poncho	C.	oposum	13.____
	D.	melee	E.	NONE MISSPELLED			
14.	A.	semester	B.	quadrent	C.	penchant	14.____
	D.	mustang	E.	NONE MISSPELLED			
15.	A.	rhetoric	B.	polygimy	C.	optimum	15.____
	D.	mendicant	E.	NONE MISSPELLED			
16.	A.	labyrint	B.	hegira	C.	ergot	16.____
	D.	debenture	E.	NONE MISSPELLED			
17.	A.	solvant	B.	radioactive	C.	photostat	17.____
	D.	nominative	E.	NONE MISSPELLED			

2 (#12)

18. A. sporadic B. excelsior C. tenible 18.____
    D. thorax   E. *NONE MISSPELLED*

19. A. mischievous B. bouillon C. asinine 19.____
    D. alien   E. *NONE MISSPELLED*

20. A. sanguinery B. prolix C. harangue 20.____
    D. minutia   E. *NONE MISSPELLED*

KEY (CORRECT ANSWERS)

1. C. abductor
2. D. consensus
3. B. propensity
4. D. ductile
5. B. superlative
6. B. appellate
7. D. debility
8. E. None Misspelled
9. A. invidious
10. A. dyspeptic
11. A. spigot
12. B. anthropology
13. C. opossum
14. B. quadrant
15. B. polygamy
16. A. labyrinth
17. A. solvent
18. C. tenable
19. E. None Misspelled
20. A. sanguinary

TEST 13

DIRECTIONS: In each of the following tests in this part, select the letter of the one MISSPELLED word in each of the following groups of words. If no word is misspelled, select the last item, letter E (none misspelled). *PRINT THE LETTER OF THE CORRECT ANSWER IN THE SPACE AT THE RIGHT.*

1. A. controvert B. cache C. auricle 1.____
   D. impromptu E. NONE MISSPELLED

2. A. labial B. heffer C. intrigue 2.____
   D. decagon E. NONE MISSPELLED

3. A. statistics B. syllable C. tenon 3.____
   D. tituler E. NONE MISSPELLED

4. A. lenient B. migraine C. embarras 4.____
   D. nepotism E. NONE MISSPELLED

5. A. lichen B. horoscope C. orthadox 5.____
   D. pageant E. NONE MISSPELLED

6. A. libretto B. humis C. fallacy 6.____
   D. dextrose E. NONE MISSPELLED

7. A. clinical B. alimoney C. bourgeois 7.____
   D. proverbial E. NONE MISSPELLED

8. A. dictator B. clipper C. braggadoccio 8.____
   D. assuage E. NONE MISSPELLED

9. A. reverence B. hydraulic C. felon 9.____
   D. diaphram E. NONE MISSPELLED

10. A. retrobution B. polyp C. optician 10.____
    D. mentor E. NONE MISSPELLED

11. A. resonant B. helicopter C. rejoicing 11.____
    D. decisive E. NONE MISSPELLED

12. A. renigade B. restitution C. faculty 12.____
    D. devise E. NONE MISSPELLED

13. A. solicitors B. gratuitous C. spherical 13.____
    D. crusible E. NONE MISSPELLED

14. A. spongy B. ramify C. pica 14.____
    D. noxtious E. NONE MISSPELLED

15. A. automaton B. cadence C. consummate 15.____
    D. ancillery E. NONE MISSPELLED

16. A. magnanimous B. iminent C. tonsillitis 16.____
    D. dowager E. NONE MISSPELLED

17. A. aerial B. apprehend C. bilinear 17.____
    D. transum E. NONE MISSPELLED

18. A. vacuum B. idiom C. veriety 18.____
    D. warbler E. *NONE MISSPELLED*

19. A. zephyr B. rarify C. physiology 19.____
    D. nonpareil E. *NONE MISSPELLED*

20. A. risque B. posterity C. opus 20.____
    D. meridian E. *NONE MISSPELLED*

KEY (CORRECT ANSWERS)

1. E. None Misspelled
2. B. heifer
3. D. titular
4. C. embarrass
5. C. orthodox
6. B. humus
7. B. alimony
8. C. braggadocio
9. D. diaphragm
10. A. retribution
11. E. None Misspelled
12. A. renegade
13. D. crucible
14. D. noxious
15. D. ancillary
16. B. imminent
17. D. transom
18. C. variety
19. B. rarefy
20. D. meridian

TEST 14

DIRECTIONS: In each of the following tests in this part, select the letter of the one MIS-SPELLED word in each of the following groups of words. If no word is misspelled, select the last item, letter E (none misspelled). *PRINT THE LETTER OF THE CORRECT ANSWER IN THE SPACE AT THE RIGHT.*

1.	A. pygmy	B. seggregation	C. clayey	1.____
	D. homogeneous	E. NONE MISSPELLED		
2.	A. homeopathy	B. predelection	C. hindrance	2.____
	D. guillotine	E. NONE MISSPELLED		
3.	A. cumulative	B. dandelion	C. incission	3.____
	D. malpractice	E. NONE MISSPELLED		
4.	A. paradise	B. allegiance	C. frustrate	4.____
	D. impecunious	E. NONE MISSPELLED		
5.	A. licquor	B. mousse	C. exclamatory	5.____
	D. disciple	E. NONE MISSPELLED		
6.	A. lame	B. winesome	C. valvular	6.____
	D. unadvised	E. NONE MISSPELLED		
7.	A. Terre Haute	B. Cyrano de Bergerac	C. Stamboul	7.____
	D. Roosvelt	E. NONE MISSPELLED		
8.	A. perambulator	B. ruminate	C. litturgy	8.____
	D. staple	E. NONE MISSPELLED		
9.	A. hectic	B. inpregnate	C. otter	9.____
	D. muscat	E. NONE MISSPELLED		
10.	A. lighterage	B. lumbar	C. insurence	10.____
	D. monsoon	E. NONE MISSPELLED		
11.	A. lethal	B. iliterateness	C. manifold	11.____
	D. minuet	E. NONE MISSPELLED		
12.	A. forfeit	B. halve	C. hundredth	12.____
	D. illusion	E. NONE MISSPELLED		
13.	A. dissolute	B. conundrum	C. fallacious	13.____
	D. descrimination	E. NONE MISSPELLED		
14.	A. diva	B. codicile	C. expedient	14.____
	D. garrison	E. NONE MISSPELLED		
15.	A. filial	B. arras	C. pantomine	15.____
	D. filament	E. NONE MISSPELLED		
16.	A. inveigle	B. paraphenalia	C. archivist	16.____
	D. complexion	E. NONE MISSPELLED		
17.	A. dessicate	B. ambidextrous	C. meritorious	17.____
	D. revocable	E. NONE MISSPELLED		

18. A. queue B. isthmus C. committal 18.____
    D. binnocular E. *NONE MISSPELLED*

19. A. changeable B. abbreviating C. regretable 19.____
    D. japanned E. *NONE MISSPELLED*

20. A. Saskechewan B. Bismarck C. Albuquerque 20.____
    D. Apennines E. *NONE MISSPELLED*

KEY (CORRECT ANSWERS)

1. B. segregation
2. B. predilection
3. C. incision
4. E. None Misspelled
5. A. liquor
6. B. winsome
7. D. Roosevelt
8. C. liturgy
9. B. impregnate
10. C. insurance
11. B. illiterateness
12. E. None Misspelled
13. D. discrimination
14. B. codicil
15. C. pantomime
16. B. paraphernalia
17. A. desiccate
18. D. binocular
19. C. regrettable
20. A. Saskatchewan

TEST 15

DIRECTIONS: In each of the following tests in this part, select the letter of the one MISSPELLED word in each of the following groups of words. If no word is misspelled, select the last item, letter E (none misspelled). *PRINT THE LETTER OF THE CORRECT ANSWER IN THE SPACE AT THE RIGHT.*

1. A. culinery B. millinery C. humpbacked 1.____
   D. improvise E. NONE MISSPELLED

2. A. Brittany B. embarrassment C. coifure 2.____
   D. leveled E. NONE MISSPELLED

3. A. minnion B. aborgine C. antagonism 3.____
   D. arabesque E. NONE MISSPELLED

4. A. tractible B. camouflage C. permanent 4.____
   D. dextrous E. NONE MISSPELLED

5. A. inequitous B. kilowatt C. weasel 5.____
   D. lunging E. NONE MISSPELLED

6. A. palatable B. odious C. motif 6.____
   D. Maltese E. NONE MISSPELLED

7. A. Beau Brummel B. Febuary C. Bedouin 7.____
   D. Damascus E. NONE MISSPELLED

8. A. llama B. madrigal C. illitive 8.____
   D. marlin E. NONE MISSPELLED

9. A. babboon B. dossier C. esplanade 9.____
   D. frontispiece E. NONE MISSPELLED

10. A. thrashing B. threshing C. atavism 10.____
    D. artifect E. NONE MISSPELLED

11. A. ballast B. ballustrade C. allotment 11.____
    D. bourgeois E. NONE MISSPELLED

12. A. amenuensis B. saccharine C. hippopotamus 12.____
    D. rhinoceros E. NONE MISSPELLED

13. A. maintenance B. bullion C. khaki 13.____
    D. libarian E. NONE MISSPELLED

14. A. diverse B. pedantic C. mishapen 14.____
    D. transient E. NONE MISSPELLED

15. A. exhilirate B. avaunt C. avocado 15.____
    D. avocation E. NONE MISSPELLED

16. A. narcotic B. flippancy C. daffodil 16.____
    D. narcisus E. NONE MISSPELLED

17. A. inflamation B. disfranchisement C. surmise 17.____
    D. adviser E. NONE MISSPELLED

121

18. A. syphon B. inquiry C. shanghaied 18.____
    D. collapsible E. *NONE MISSPELLED*

19. A. occassionally B. antecedence C. reprehensible 19.____
    D. inveigh E. *NONE MISSPELLED*

20. A. crescendos B. indispensible C. mosquitoes 20.____
    D. impeccable E. *NONE MISSPELLED*

KEY (CORRECT ANSWERS)

1. A. culinary
2. C. coiffure
3. A. minion
4. A. tractable
5. A. iniquitous
6. E. None Misspelled
7. B. February
8. D. illative
9. A. baboon
10. D. artifact
11. B. balustrade
12. A. amanuensis
13. D. librarian
14. C. misshapen
15. A. exhilarate
16. D. narcissus
17. A. inflammation
18. E. None Misspelled
19. A. occasionally
20. B. indispensable

EXAMINATION SECTION
TEST 1

DIRECTIONS: Each question or incomplete statement is followed by several suggested answers or completions. Select the one that BEST answers the question or completes the statement. *PRINT THE LETTER OF THE CORRECT ANSWER IN THE SPACE AT THE RIGHT.*

1. A supervisor may be required to help train a newly appointed clerk.
   Which of the following is LEAST important for a newly appointed clerk to know in order to perform his work efficiently?

   A. Acceptable ways of answering and recording telephone calls
   B. The number of files in the storage files unit
   C. The filing methods used by his unit
   D. Proper techniques for handling visitors

   1.____

2. In your agency you have the responsibility of processing clients who have appointments with agency representatives. On a particularly busy day, a client comes to your desk and insists that she must see the person handling her case although she has no appointment.
   Under the circumstances, your FIRST action should be to

   A. show her the full appointment schedule
   B. give her an appointment for another day
   C. ask her to explain the urgency
   D. tell her to return later in the day

   2.____

3. Which of the following practices is BEST for a supervisor to use when assigning work to his staff?

   A. Give workers with seniority the most difficult jobs
   B. Assign all unimportant work to the slower workers
   C. Permit each employee to pick the job he prefers
   D. Make assignments based on the workers' abilities

   3.____

4. In which of the following instances is a supervisor MOST justified in giving commands to people under his supervision? When

   A. they delay in following instructions which have been given to them clearly
   B. they become relaxed and slow about work, and he wants to speed up their production
   C. he must direct them in an emergency situation
   D. he is instructing them on jobs that are unfamiliar to them

   4.____

5. Which of the following supervisory actions or attitudes is MOST likely to result in getting subordinates to try to do as much work as possible for a supervisor?
   He

   A. shows that his most important interest is in schedules and production goals
   B. consistently pressures his staff to get the work out
   C. never fails to let them know he is in charge
   D. considers their abilities and needs while requiring that production goals be met

   5.____

6. Assume that a supervisor has been explaining certain regulations to a new clerk under his supervision.
   The MOST efficient way for the supervisor to make sure that the clerk has understood the explanation is to

   A. give him written materials on the regulations
   B. ask him if he has any further questions about the regulations
   C. ask him specific questions based on what has just been explained to him
   D. watch the way he handles a situation involving these regulations

7. One of your unit clerks has been assigned to work for a Mr. Jones in another office for several days. At the end of the first day, Mr. Jones, saying the clerk was not satisfactory, asks that she not be assigned to him again. This clerk is one of your most dependable workers, and no previous complaints about her work have come to you from any other outside assignments.
   To get to the root of this situation, your FIRST action should be to

   A. ask Mr. Jones to explain in what way her work was unsatisfactory
   B. ask the clerk what she did that Mr. Jones considered unsatisfactory
   C. check with supervisors for whom she previously worked to see if your own rating of her is in error
   D. tell Mr. Jones to pick the clerk he would prefer to have work for him the next time

8. A senior typist, still on probation, is instructed to type, as quickly as possible, one section of a draft of a long, complex report. Her part must be typed and readable before another part of the report can be written. Asked when she can have the report ready, she gives her supervisor an estimate of a day longer than she knows it will actually take. She then finishes the job a day sooner than the date given her supervisor.
   The judgment shown by the senior typist in giving an overestimate of time in a situation like this is, in general,

   A. *good* because it prevents the supervisor from thinking she works slowly
   B. *good* because it keeps unrealistic supervisors from expecting too much
   C. *bad* because she should have used the time left to further check and proofread her work
   D. *bad* because schedules and plans for other parts of the project may have been based on her false estimate

9. Suppose a new clerk, still on probation, is placed under your supervision and refuses to do a job you ask him to do. What is the FIRST thing you should do?

   A. Explain that you are the supervisor and he must follow your instructions.
   B. Tell him he may be suspended if he refuses.
   C. Ask someone else to do the job and rate him accordingly.
   D. Ask for his reason for objecting to the request.

10. As a supervisor of a small group of people, you have blamed worker A for something that you later find out was really done by worker B.
    The BEST thing for you to do now would be to

A. say nothing to worker A but criticize worker B for his mistake while worker A is near so that A will realize that you know who made the mistake
B. speak to each worker separately, apologize to worker A for your mistake, and discuss worker B's mistake with him
C. bring both workers together, apologize to worker A for your mistake, and discuss worker B's mistake with him
D. say nothing now but be careful about mixing up worker A with worker B in the future

11. You have just learned one of your staff is grumbling that she thinks you are not pleased with her work. As far as you're concerned, this isn't true at all. In fact, you've paid no particular attention to this worker lately because you've been very busy. You have just finished preparing an important report and *breaking in* a new clerk.
Under the circumstances, the BEST thing to do is

A. ignore her; after all, it's just a figment of her imagination
B. discuss the matter with her now to try to find out and eliminate the cause of this problem
C. tell her not to worry about it; you haven't had time to think about her work
D. make a note to meet with her at a later date in order to straighten out the situation

11.____

12. A most important job of a supervisor is to positively motivate employees to increase their work production. Which of the following LEAST indicates that a group of workers has been positively motivated?

A. Their work output becomes constant and stable.
B. Their cooperation at work becomes greater.
C. They begin to show pride in the product of their work.
D. They show increased interest in their work.

12.____

13. Which of the following traits would be LEAST important in considering a person for a merit increase?

A. Punctuality   B. Using initiative successfully
C. High rate of production   D. Resourcefulness

13.____

14. Of the following, the action LEAST likely to gain a supervisor the cooperation of his staff is for him to

A. give each person consideration as an individual
B. be as objective as possible when evaluating work performance
C. rotate the least popular assignments
D. expect subordinates to be equally competent

14.____

15. It has been said that, for the supervisor, nothing can beat the *face-to-face* communication of talking to one subordinate at a time.
This method is, however, LEAST appropriate to use when the

A. supervisor is explaining a change in general office procedure
B. subject is of personal importance
C. supervisor is conducting a yearly performance evaluation of all employees
D. supervisor must talk to some of his employees concerning their poor attendance and punctuality

15.____

16. While you are on the telephone answering a question about your agency, a visitor comes to your desk and starts to ask you a question. There is no emergency or urgency in either situation, that of the phone call or that of answering the visitor's question.
In this case, you should

   A. continue to answer the person on the telephone until you are finished and then tell the visitor you are sorry to have kept him waiting
   B. excuse yourself to the person on the telephone and tell the visitor that you will be with him as soon as you have finished on the phone
   C. explain to the person on the telephone that you have a visitor and must shorten the conversation
   D. continue to answer the person on the phone while looking up occasionally at the visitor to let him know that you know he is waiting

17. While speaking on the telephone to someone who called, you are disconnected.
The FIRST thing you should do is

   A. hang up but try to keep your line free to receive the call back
   B. immediately get the dialtone and continually dial the person who called you until you reach him
   C. signal the switchboard operator and ask her to re-establish the connection
   D. dial 0 for Operator and explain that you were disconnected

18. The type of speech used by an office worker in telephone conversations greatly affects the communicator.
Of the following, the BEST way to express your ideas when telephoning is with a vocabulary that consists mainly of _____ words.

   A. formal, intellectual sounding
   B. often used colloquial
   C. technical, emphatic
   D. simple, descriptive

19. Suppose a clerk under your supervision has taken a personal phone call and is at the same time needed to answer a question regarding an assignment being handled by another member of your office. He appears confused as to what he should do. How should you instruct him later as to how to handle a similar situation?
You should tell him to

   A. tell the caller to hold on while he answers the question
   B. tell the caller to call back a little later
   C. return the call during an assigned break
   D. finish the conversation quickly and answer the question

20. You are asked to place a telephone call by your supervisor. When you place the call, you receive what appears to be a wrong number.
Of the following, you should FIRST

   A. check the number with your supervisor to see if the number he gave you is correct
   B. ask the person on the other end what his number is and who he is
   C. check with the person on the other end to see if the number you dialed is the number you received
   D. apologize to the person on the other end for disturbing him and hang up

Questions 21-30.

WORD MEANING

DIRECTIONS: Each Question 21 through 30 contains a word in capitals followed by four suggested meanings of the word. For each question, choose the BEST meaning and write the letter of the best meaning in the space at the right.

21. ACCURATE 21.____
 A. correct   B. useful   C. afraid   D. careless

22. ALTER 22.____
 A. copy   B. change   C. repeat   D. agree

23. DOCUMENT 23.____
 A. outline   B. agreement   C. blueprint   D. record

24. INDICATE 24.____
 A. listen   B. show   C. guess   D. try

25. INVENTORY 25.____
 A. custom   B. discovery   C. warning   D. list

26. ISSUE 26.____
 A. annoy   B. use up   C. give out   D. gain

27. NOTIFY 27.____
 A. inform   B. promise   C. approve   D. strengthen

28. ROUTINE 28.____
 A. path   B. mistake   C. habit   D. journey

29. TERMINATE 29.____
 A. rest   B. start   C. deny   D. end

30. TRANSMIT 30.____
 A. put in   B. send   C. stop   D. go across

Questions 31-35.

READING COMPREHENSION

DIRECTIONS: Questions 31 through 35 test how well you understand what you read. It will be necessary for you to read carefully because your answers to these questions should be based SOLELY on the information given in the following paragraphs.

The recipient gains an impression of a typewritten letter before he begins to read the message. Factors which provide for a good first impression include margins and spacing that are visually pleasing, formal parts of the letter which are correctly placed according to the style of the letter, copy which is free of obvious erasures and over-strikes, and transcript that is even and clear. The problem for the typist is that of how to produce that first, positive impression of her work.

There are several general rules which a typist can follow when she wishes to prepare a properly spaced letter on a sheet of letterhead. Ordinarily, the width of a letter should not be less the four inches nor more than six inches. The side margins should also have a desirable relation to the bottom margin and the space between the letterhead and the body of the letter. Usually the most appealing arrangement is when the side margins are even and the bottom margin is slightly wider than the side margins. In some offices, however, standard line length is used for all business letters, and the secretary then varies the spacing between the date line and the inside address according to the length of the letter.

31. The BEST title for the above paragraphs would be:

    A. Writing Office Letters
    B. Making Good First Impressions
    C. Judging Well-Typed Letters
    D. Good Placing and Spacing for Office Letters

32. According to the above paragraphs, which of the following might be considered the way in which people very quickly judge the quality of work which has been typed?
    By

    A. measuring the margins to see if they are correct
    B. looking at the spacing and cleanliness of the typescript
    C. scanning the body of the letter for meaning
    D. reading the date line and address for errors

33. What, according to the above paragraphs, would be definitely UNDESIRABLE as the average line length of a typed letter?

    A. 4"   B. 5"   C. 6"   D. 7"

34. According to the above paragraphs, when the line length is kept standard, the secretary

    A. does not have to vary the spacing at all since this also is standard
    B. adjusts the spacing between the date line and inside address for different lengths of letters
    C. uses the longest line as a guideline for spacing between the date line and inside address
    D. varies the number of spaces between the lines

35. According to the above paragraphs, side margins are MOST pleasing when they

    A. are even and somewhat smaller than the bottom margin
    B. are slightly wider than the bottom margin
    C. vary with the length of the letter
    D. are figured independently from the letterhead and the body of the letter

Questions 36-40.

CODING

DIRECTIONS: Name of Applicant   H A N G S B R U K E
               Test Code   c o m p l e x i t y
               File Number   0 1 2 3 4 5 6 7 8 9

Assume that each of the above capital letters is the first letter of the name of an applicant, that the small letter directly beneath each capital letter is the test code for the applicant, and that the number directly beneath each code letter is the file number for the applicant.

In each of the following Questions 36 through 40, the test code letters and the file numbers in Columns 2 and 3 should correspond to the capital letters in Column 1. For each question, look at each Column carefully and mark your answer as follows:

If there is an error only in Column 2, mark your answer A.
If there is an error only in Column 3, mark your answer B.
If there is an error in both Columns 2 and 3, mark your answer C.
If both Columns 2 and 3 are correct, mark your answer D.

The following sample question is given to help you understand the procedure.

SAMPLE QUESTION

Column 1	Column 2	Column 3
AKEHN	otyci	18902

In Column 2, the final test code letter *i* should be *m*. Column 3 is correctly coded to Column 1. Since there is an error only in Column 2, the answer is A.

	Column 1	Column 2	Column 3	
36.	NEKKU	mytti	29987	36.____
37.	KRAEB	txlye	86095	37.____
38.	ENAUK	ymoit	92178	38.____
39.	REANA	xeomo	69121	39.____
40.	EKHSE	ytcxy	97049	40.____

Questions 41-50.

ARITHMETICAL REASONING

DIRECTIONS: Solve the following problems.

41. If a secretary answered 28 phone calls and typed the addresses for 112 credit statements in one morning, what is the RATIO of phone calls answered to credit statements typed for that period of time?   41.____

     A. 1:4   B. 1:7   C. 2:3   D. 3:5

42. According to a suggested filing system, no more than 10 folders should be filed behind any one file guide, and from 15 to 25 file guides should be used in each file drawer for easy finding and filing.
The MAXIMUM number of folders that a five-drawer file cabinet can hold to allow easy finding and filing is

   A. 550   B. 750   C. 1,100   D. 1,250

43. An employee had a starting salary of $32,902. He received a salary increase at the end of each year, and at the end of the seventh year, his salary was $36,738. What was his AVERAGE annual increase in salary over these seven years?

   A. $510   B. $538   C. $548   D. $572

44. The 55 typists and 28 senior clerks in a certain agency were paid a total of $1,943,200 in salaries for the year. If the average annual salary of a typist was $22,400, the AVERAGE annual salary of a senior clerk was

   A. $25,400   B. $26,600   C. $26,800   D. $27,000

45. A typist has been given a three-page report to type. She has finished typing the first two pages. The first page has 283 words, and the second page has 366 words.
If the total report consists of 954 words, how many words will she have to type on the third page of the report?

   A. 202   B. 287   C. 305   D. 313

46. In one day, Clerk A processed 30% more forms than Clerk B, and Clerk C processed 1 1/4 as many forms as Clerk A.
If Clerk B processed 40 forms, how many MORE forms were processed by Clerk C than Clerk B?

   A. 12   B. 13   C. 21   D. 25

47. A clerk who earns a gross salary of $452 every week has the following deductions taken from her paycheck: 17 1/2% for City, State, Federal taxes, and for Social Security, $1.20 for health insurance, and $6.10 for union dues. The amount of her take-home pay is

   A. $286.40   B. $312.40   C. $331.60   D. $365.60

48. In 2006 an agency spent $200 to buy pencils at a cost of $1 a dozen.
If the agency used 3/4 of these pencils in 2006 and used the same number of pencils in 2007, how many MORE pencils did it have to buy to have enough pencils for all of 2007?

   A. 1,200   B. 2,400   C. 3,600   D. 4,800

49. A clerk who worked in Agency X earned the following salaries: $30,070 the first year, $30,500 the second year, and $30,960 the third year. Another clerk who worked in Agency Y for three years earned $30,550 a year for two years and $30,724 the third year.
The DIFFERENCE between the average salaries received by both clerks over a three-year period is

   A. $98   B. $102   C. $174   D. $282

50. An employee who works over 40 hours in any week receives overtime payment for the extra hours at time and one-half (1 1/2 times) his hourly rate of pay. An employee who earns $7.80 an hour works a total of 45 hours during a certain week.
His TOTAL pay for that week would be

   A. $312.00   B. $351.00   C. $370.50   D. $412.00

50.____

KEY (CORRECT ANSWERS)

1. B	11. B	21. A	31. D	41. A
2. C	12. A	22. B	32. B	42. D
3. D	13. A	23. D	33. D	43. C
4. C	14. D	24. B	34. B	44. A
5. D	15. A	25. D	35. A	45. C
6. C	16. B	26. C	36. B	46. D
7. A	17. A	27. A	37. C	47. D
8. D	18. D	28. C	38. D	48. B
9. D	19. C	29. D	39. A	49. A
10. B	20. C	30. B	40. C	50. C

TEST 2

DIRECTIONS: Each question or incomplete statement is followed by several suggested answers or completions. Select the one that BEST answers the question or completes the statement. *PRINT THE LETTER OF THE CORRECT ANSWER IN THE SPACE AT THE RIGHT.*

1. To tell a newly employed clerk to fill a top drawer of a four-drawer cabinet with heavy folders which will be often used and to keep lower drawers only partly filled is

    A. *good* because a tall person would have to bend unnecessarily if he had to use a lower drawer
    B. *bad* because the file cabinet may tip over when the top drawer is opened
    C. *good* because it is the most easily reachable drawer for the average person
    D. *bad* because a person bending down at another drawer may accidentally bang his head on the bottom of the drawer when he straightens up

1.____

2. If you have requisitioned a *ream* of paper in order to duplicate a single page office announcement, how many announcements can be printed from the one package of paper?

    A. 200   B. 500   C. 700   D. 1,000

2.____

3. In the operations of a government agency, a voucher is ORDINARILY used to

    A. refer someone to the agency for a position or assignment
    B. certify that an agency's records of financial transactions are accurate
    C. order payment from agency funds of a stated amount to an individual
    D. enter a statement of official opinion in the records of the agency

3.____

4. Of the following types of cards used in filing systems, the one which is generally MOST helpful in locating records which might be filed under more than one subject is the _____ card.

    A. cut   B. tickler
    C. cross-reference D. visible index

4.____

5. The type of filing system in which one does NOT need to refer to a card index in order to find the folder is called

    A. alphabetic   B. geographic   C. subject   D. locational

5.____

6. Of the following, records management is LEAST concerned with

    A. the development of the best method for retrieving important information
    B. deciding what records should be kept
    C. deciding the number of appointments a client will need
    D. determining the types of folders to be used

6.____

7. If records are continually removed from a set of files without *charging* them to the borrower, the filing system will soon become ineffective.
Of the following terms, the one which is NOT applied to a form used in a charge-out system is a

    A. requisition card   B. out-folder
    C. record retrieval form D. substitution card

7.____

8. A new clerk has been told to put 500 cards in alphabetical order. Another clerk suggests that she divide the cards into four groups such as A to F, G to L, M to R, and S to Z, and then alphabetize these four smaller groups.
The suggested method is

   A. *poor* because the clerk will have to handle the sheets more than once and will waste time
   B. *good* because it saves time, is more accurate, and is less tiring
   C. *good* because she will not have to concentrate on it so much when it is in smaller groups
   D. *poor* because this method is much more tiring than straight alphabetizing

8._____

9. The term that describes the equipment attached to an office computer is

   A. interface   B. network   C. hardware   D. software

9._____

10. Suppose a clerk has been given pads of pre-printed forms to use when taking phone messages for others in her office. The clerk is then observed using scraps of paper and not the forms for writing her messages.
It should be explained that the BEST reason for using the forms is that

   A. they act as a checklist to make sure that the important information is taken
   B. she is expected to do her work in the same way as others in the office
   C. they make sure that unassigned paper is not wasted on phone messages
   D. learning to use these forms will help train her to use more difficult forms

10._____

11. Of the following, the one which is spelled incorrectly is

   A. alphabetization   B. reccommendation
   C. redaction   D. synergy

11._____

12. Of the following, the MAIN reason a stock clerk keeps a perpetual inventory of supplies in the storeroom is that such an inventory will

   A. eliminate the need for a physical inventory
   B. provide a continuous record of supplies on hand
   C. indicate whether a shipment of supplies is satisfactory
   D. dictate the terms of the purchase order

12._____

13. As a supervisor, you may be required to handle different types of correspondence.
Of the following types of letters, it would be MOST important to promptly seal which kind of letters?

   A. One marked *confidential*
   B. Those containing enclosures
   C. Any letter to be sent airmail
   D. Those in which carbons will be sent along with the original

13._____

14. While opening incoming mail, you notice that one letter indicates that an enclosure was to be included but, even after careful inspection, you are not able to find the information to which this refers.
Of the following, the thing that you should do FIRST is

14._____

A. replace the letter in its envelope and return it to the sender
B. file the letter until the sender's office mails the missing information
C. type out a letter to the sender informing them of their error
D. make a notation in the margin of the letter that the enclosure was omitted

15. You have been given a checklist and assigned the responsibility of inspecting certain equipment in the various offices of your agency.
Which of the following is the GREATEST advantage of the checklist?

    A. It indicates which equipment is in greatest demand.
    B. Each piece of equipment on the checklist will be checked only once.
    C. It helps to insure that the equipment listed will not be overlooked.
    D. The equipment listed suggests other equipment you should look for.

16. Your supervisor has asked you to locate a telephone number for an attorney named Jones, whose office is located at 311 Broadway and whose name is not already listed in your files.
The BEST method for finding the number would be for you to

    A. call the information operator and have her get it for you
    B. look in the alphabetical directory (white pages) under the name Jones at 311 Broadway
    C. refer to the heading Attorney in the yellow pages for the name Jones at 311 Broadway
    D. ask your supervisor who referred her to Mr. Jones, then call that person for the number

17. An example of material that should NOT be sent by first class mail is a

    A. carbon copy of a letter   B. postcard
    C. business reply card   D. large catalogue

18. Which of the following BEST describes *office work simplification?*

    A. An attempt to increase the rate of production by speeding up the movements of employees
    B. Eliminating wasteful steps in order to increase efficiency
    C. Making jobs as easy as possible for employees so they will not be overworked
    D. Eliminating all difficult tasks from an office and leaving only simple ones

19. The duties of a supervisor who is assigned the job of timekeeper may include all of the following EXCEPT

    A. computing and recording regular hours worked each day in accordance with the normal work schedule
    B. approving requests for vacation leave, sick leave, and annual leave
    C. computing and recording overtime hours worked beyond the normal schedule
    D. determining the total regular hours and total extra hours worked during the week

20. Suppose a clerk under your supervision accidentally opens a personal letter while handling office mail.
Under such circumstances, you should tell the clerk to put the letter back into the envelope and

A. take the letter to the person to whom it belongs and make sure he understands that the clerk did not read it
B. try to seal the envelope so it won't appear to have been opened
C. write on the envelope *Sorry - opened by mistake,* and put his initials on it
D. write on the envelope *Sorry - opened by mistake,* but not put his initials on it

Questions 21-25.

SPELLING

DIRECTIONS: Each Question 21 through 25 consists of three words. In each question, one of the words may be spelled incorrectly or all three may be spelled correctly. For each question, if one of the words is spelled incorrectly, write the letter of the incorrect word in the space at the right. If all three words are spelled correctly, write the letter D in the space at the right.

SAMPLE I: (A) guide (B) departmint (C) stranger

SAMPLE II: (A) comply (B) valuable (C) window

In the Sample Question I, *departmint* is incorrect.
It should be spelled *department.* Therefore, B is the answer to Sample Question I.
In the Sample Question II, all three words are spelled correctly. Therefore, D is the answer to Sample Question II.

21.	A. argument	B. reciept	C. complain	21._____
22.	A. sufficient	B. postpone	C. visible	22._____
23.	A. expirience	B. dissatisfy	C. alternate	23._____
24.	A. occurred	B. noticable	C. appendix	24._____
25.	A. anxious	B. guarantee	C. calender	25._____

Questions 26-30.

ENGLISH USAGE

DIRECTIONS: Each Question 26 through 30 contains a sentence. Read each sentence carefully to decide whether it is correct. Then, in the space at the right, mark your answer:
(A) if the sentence is incorrect because of bad grammar or sentence structure
(B) if the sentence is incorrect because of bad punctuation
(C) if the sentence is incorrect because of bad capitalization
(D) if the sentence is correct

Each incorrect sentence has only one type of error. Consider a sentence correct if it has no errors, although there may be other correct ways of saying the same thing.

SAMPLE QUESTION I: One of our clerks were promoted yesterday.

The subject of this sentence is *one,* so the verb should be *was promoted* instead of *were promoted.* Since the sentence is incorrect because of bad grammar, the answer to Sample Question I is A.

SAMPLE QUESTION II: Between you and me, I would prefer not going there.

Since this sentence is correct, the answer to Sample Question II is D.

26. The National alliance of Businessmen is trying to persuade private businesses to hire youth in the summertime. 26.____

27. The supervisor who is on vacation, is in charge of processing vouchers. 27.____

28. The activity of the committee at its conferences is always stimulating. 28.____

29. After checking the addresses again, the letters went to the mailroom. 29.____

30. The director, as well as the employees, are interested in sharing the dividends. 30.____

Questions 31-40.

FILING

DIRECTIONS: Each Question 31 through 40 contains four names. For each question, choose the name that should be FIRST if the four names are to be arranged in alphabetical order in accordance with the Rules for Alphabetical Filing given below. Read these rules carefully. Then, for each question, indicate in the correspondingly numbered space at the right the letter before the name that should be FIRST in alphabetical order.

RULES FOR ALPHABETICAL FILING

Names of People

(1) The names of people are filed in strict alphabetical order, first according to the last name, then according to first name or initial, and finally according to middle name or initial. For example: George Allen comes before Edward Bell, and Leonard P. Reston comes before Lucille B. Reston.

(2) When last names are the same, for example A. Green and Agnes Green, the one with the initial comes before the one with the name written out when the first initials are identical.

(3) When first and last names are alike and the middle name is given, for example John David Doe and John Devoe Doe, the names should be filed in the alphabetical order of the middle names.

(4) When first and last names are the same, a name without a middle initial comes before one with a middle name or initial. For example: John Doe comes before both John A. Doe and John Alan Doe.

(5) When first and last names are the same, a name with a middle initial comes before one with a middle name beginning with the same initial. For example: Jack R. Herts comes before Jack Richard Hertz.

(6) Prefixes such as De, 0', Mac, Mc, and Van are filed as written and are treated as part of the names to which they are connected. For example: Robert O'Dea is filed before David Olsen.

(7) Abbreviated names are treated as if they were spelled out. For example: Chas. is filed as Charles and Thos. is filed as Thomas.

(8) Titles and designations such as Dr., Mr., and Prof, are disregarded in filing.

<u>Names of Organizations</u>

(1) The names of business organizations are filed according to the order in which each word in the name appears. When an organization name bears the name of a person, it is filed according to the rules for filing names of people as given above. For example: William Smith Service Co. comes before Television Distributors, Inc.

(2) Where bureau, board, office or department appears as the first part of the title of a governmental agency, that agency should be filed under the word in the title expressing the chief function of the agency. For example: Bureau of the Budget would be filed as if written Budget, (Bureau of the). The Department of Personnel would be filed as if written Personnel, (Department of).

(3) When the following words are part of an organization, they are disregarded: the, of, and.

(4) When there are numbers in a name, they are treated as if they were spelled out. For example: 10th Street Bootery is filed as Tenth Street Bootery.

SAMPLE QUESTION: (A) Jane Earl   (2)
                  (B) James A. Earle (4)
                  (C) James Earl   (1)
                  (D) J. Earle   (3)

The numbers in parentheses show the proper alphabetical order in which these names should be filed. Since the name that should be filed FIRST is James Earl, the answer to the sample question is C.

31. A. Majorca Leather Goods
     B. Robert Maiorca and Sons
     C. Maintenance Management Corp.
     D. Majestic Carpet Mills

32. A. Municipal Telephone Service
    B. Municipal Reference Library
    C. Municipal Credit Union
    D. Municipal Broadcasting System

33. A. Robert B. Pierce   B. R. Bruce Pierce
    C. Ronald Pierce   D. Robert Bruce Pierce

34. A. Four Seasons Sports Club
    B. 14 Street Shopping Center
    C. Forty Thieves Restaurant
    D. 42nd St. Theaters

35. A. Franco Franceschini   B. Amos Franchini
    C. Sandra Franceschia   D. Lilie Franchinesca

36. A. Chas. A. Levine   B. Kurt Levene
    C. Charles Levine   D. Kurt E. Levene

37. A. Prof. Geo. Kinkaid   B. Mr. Alan Kinkaid
    C. Dr. Albert A. Kinkade D. Kincade Liquors Inc.

38. A. Department of Public Events
    B. Office of the Public Administrator
    C. Queensborough Public Library
    D. Department of Public Health

39. A. Martin Luther King, Jr. Towers
    B. Metro North Plaza
    C. Manhattanville Houses
    D. Marble Hill Houses

40. A. Dr. Arthur Davids
    B. The David Check Cashing Service
    C. A.C. Davidsen
    D. Milton Davidoff

Questions 41-45.

READING COMPREHENSION

DIRECTIONS: Questions 41 through 45 test how well you understand what you read. It will be necessary for you to read carefully because your answers to these questions should be based SOLELY on the information given in the following paragraph.

Work standards presuppose an ability to measure work. Measurement in office management is needed for several reasons. First, it is necessary to evaluate the overall efficiency of the office itself. It is then essential to measure the efficiency of each particular section or unit and that of the individual worker. To plan and control the work of sections and units, one must have measurement. A program of measurement goes hand in hand with a program of standards. One can have measurement without standards, but one cannot have work standards without measurement. Providing data on amount of work done and time expended, measure-

ment does not deal with the amount of energy expended by an individual although in many cases such energy may be in direct proportion to work output. Usually from two-thirds to three-fourths of all work can be measured. However, less than two-thirds of all work is actually measured because measurement difficulties are encountered when office work is non-repetitive and irregular, or when it is primarily mental rather than manual. These obstacles are often used as excuses for non-measurement far more frequently than is justified.

41. According to the paragraph, an office manager cannot set work standards unless he can 41._____

    A. plan the amount of work to be done
    B. control the amount of work that is done
    C. estimate accurately the quantity of work done
    D. delegate the amount of work to be done to efficient workers

42. According to the paragraph, the type of office work that would be MOST difficult to measure would be 42._____

    A. checking warrants for accuracy of information
    B. recording payroll changes
    C. processing applications
    D. making up a new system of giving out supplies

43. According to the paragraph, the actual amount of work that is measured is _____ of all work. 43._____

    A. less than two-thirds
    B. two-thirds to three-fourths
    C. less than three-sixths
    D. more than three-fourths

44. Which of the following would be MOST difficult to determine by using measurement techniques? 44._____

    A. The amount of work that is accomplished during a certain period of time
    B. The amount of work that should be planned for a period of time
    C. How much time is needed to do a certain task
    D. The amount of incentive a person must have to do his job

45. The one of the following which is the MOST suitable title for the paragraph is: 45._____

    A. How Measurement of Office Efficiency Depends on Work Standards
    B. Using Measurement for Office Management and Efficiency
    C. Work Standards and the Efficiency of the Office Worker
    D. Managing the Office Using Measured Work Standards

Questions 46-50.

INTERPRETING STATISTICAL DATA

DIRECTIONS: Answer Questions 46 through 50 using the information given in the table below.

AGE COMPOSITION IN THE LABOR FORCE IN CITY A
(1990-2000)

	Age Group	1990	1995	2000
Men	14 - 24	8,430	10,900	14,340
	25 - 44	22,200	22,350	26,065
	45+	17,550	19,800	21,970
Women	14 - 24	4,450	6,915	7,680
	25 - 44	9,080	10,010	11,550
	45+	7,325	9,470	13,180

46. The GREATEST increase in the number of people in the labor force between 1990 and 1995 occurred among

   A. men between the ages of 14 and 24
   B. men age 45 and over
   C. women between the ages of 14 and 24
   D. women age 45 and over

46.____

47. If the total number of women of all ages in the labor force increases from 2000 to 2005 by the same number as it did from 1995 to 2000, the TOTAL number of women of all ages in the labor force in 2005 will be

   A. 27,425   B. 29,675   C. 37,525   D. 38,425

47.____

48. The total increase in numbers of women in the labor force from 1990 to 1995 differs from the total increase of men in the same years by being _____ than that of men.

   A. 770 less   B. 670 more   C. 770 more   D. 1,670 more

48.____

49. In the year 1990, the proportion of married women in each group was as follows: 1/5 of the women in the 14-24 age group, 1/4 of those in the 25-44 age group, and 2/5 of those 45 and over.
How many married women were in the labor force in 1990?

   A. 4,625   B. 5,990   C. 6,090   D. 7,910

49.____

50. The 14-24 age group of men in the labor force from 1990 to 2000 increased by APPROXIMATELY

   A. 40%   B. 65%   C. 70%   D. 75%

50.____

KEY (CORRECT ANSWERS)

1. B	11. B	21. B	31. C	41. C
2. B	12. B	22. D	32. D	42. D
3. C	13. A	23. A	33. B	43. A
4. C	14. D	24. B	34. D	44. D
5. A	15. C	25. C	35. C	45. B
6. C	16. C	26. C	36. B	46. A
7. C	17. D	27. B	37. D	47. D
8. B	18. B	28. D	38. B	48. B
9. C	19. B	29. A	39. A	49. C
10. A	20. C	30. A	40. B	50. C

EXAMINATION SECTION
TEST 1

DIRECTIONS: Each question or incomplete statement is followed by several suggested answers or completions. Select the one that BEST answers the question or completes the statement. *PRINT THE LETTER OF THE CORRECT ANSWER IN THE SPACE AT THE RIGHT.*

Questions 1-4.

DIRECTIONS: Answer Questions 1 through 4 SOLELY on the basis of the following passage.

Job analysis combined with performance appraisal is an excellent method of determining training needs of individuals. The steps in this method are to determine the specific duties of the job, to evaluate the adequacy with which the employee performs each of these duties, and finally to determine what significant improvements can be made by training.

The list of duties can be obtained in a number of ways: asking the employee, asking the supervisor, observing the employee, etc. Adequacy of performance can be estimated by the employee, but the supervisor's evaluation must also be obtained. This evaluation will usually be based on observation.

What does the supervisor observe? The employee, while he is working; the employee's work relationships; the ease, speed, and sureness of the employee's actions; the way he applies himself to the job; the accuracy and amount of completed work; its conformity with established procedures and standards; the appearance of the work; the soundness of judgment it shows; and, finally, signs of good or poor communication, understanding, and cooperation among employees.

Such observation is a normal and inseparable part of the everyday job of supervision. Systematically, recorded, evaluated, and summarized, it highlights both general and individual training needs.

1. According to the passage, job analysis may be used by the supervisor in

    A. increasing his own understanding of tasks performed in his unit
    B. increasing efficiency of communication within the organization
    C. assisting personnel experts in the classification of positions
    D. determining in which areas an employee needs more instruction

2. According to the passage, the FIRST step in determining the training needs of employees is to

    A. locate the significant improvements that can be made by training
    B. determine the specific duties required in a job
    C. evaluate the employee's performance
    D. motivate the employee to want to improve himself

3. On the basis of the above passage, which of the following is the BEST way for a supervisor to determine the adequacy of employee performance?

    A. Check the accuracy and amount of completed work
    B. Ask the training officer
    C. Observe all aspects of the employee's work
    D. Obtain the employee's own estimate

4. Which of the following is NOT mentioned by the passage as a factor to be taken into consideration in judging the adequacy of employee performance?

   A. Accuracy of completed work
   B. Appearance of completed work
   C. Cooperation among employees
   D. Attitude of the employee toward his supervisor

5. In indexing names of business firms and other organizations, ONE of the rules to be followed is:

   A. The word *and* is considered an indexing unit
   B. When a firm name includes the full name of a person who is not well-known, the person's first name is considered as the first indexing unit
   C. Usually the units in a firm name are indexed in the order in which they are written
   D. When a firm's name is made up of single letters (such as ABC Corp.), the letters taken together are considered more than one indexing unit

6. Assume that people often come to your office with complaints of errors in your agency's handling of their clients. The employees in your office have the job of listening to these complaints and investigating them. One day, when it is almost closing time, a person comes into your office, apparently very angry, and demands that you take care of his complaint at once.
   Your IMMEDIATE reaction should be to

   A. suggest that he return the following day
   B. find out his name and the nature of his complaint
   C. tell him to write a letter
   D. call over your superior

7. Assume that part of your job is to notify people concerning whether their applications for a certain program have been approved or disapproved. However, you do not actually make the decision on approval or disapproval. One day, you answer a telephone call from a woman who states that she has not yet received any word on her application. She goes on to tell you her qualifications for the program. From what she has said, you know that persons with such qualifications are usually approved.
   Of the following, which one is the BEST thing for you to say to her?

   A. "You probably will be accepted, but wait until you receive a letter before trying to join the program."
   B. "Since you seem well qualified, I am sure that your application will be approved."
   C. "If you can write us a letter emphasizing your qualifications, it may speed up the process."
   D. "You will be notified of the results of your application as soon as a decision has been made."

8. Suppose that one of your duties includes answering specific telephone inquiries. Your superior refers a call to you from an irate person who claims that your agency is inefficient and is wasting taxpayers' money.
   Of the following, the BEST way to handle such a call is to

   A. listen briefly and then hang up without answering
   B. note the caller's comments and tell him that you will transmit them to your superiors

C. connect the caller with the head of your agency
D. discuss your own opinions with the caller

9. An employee has been assigned to open her division head's mail and place it on his desk. One day, the employee opens a letter which she then notices is marked *Personal*. Of the following, the BEST action for her to take is to

   A. write *Personal* on the letter and staple the envelope to the back of the letter
   B. ignore the matter and treat the letter the same way as the others
   C. give it to another division head to hold until her own division head comes into the office
   D. leave the letter in the envelope and write *Sorry opened by mistake* on the envelope and initial it

Questions 10-14.

DIRECTIONS: Questions 10 through 14 each consist of a quotation which contains one word that is incorrectly used because it is not in keeping with the meaning that the quotation is evidently intended to convey. Of the words underlined in each quotation, determine which word is incorrectly used. Then select from among the words lettered A, B, C, and D the word which, when substituted for the incorrectly used word, would BEST help to convey the meaning of the quotation. (Do NOT indicate a change for an underlined word unless the underlined word is incorrectly used.)

10. Unless reasonable managerial supervision is <u>exercised</u> over office supplies, it is certain that there will be extravagance, <u>rejected</u> items out of stock, <u>excessive</u> prices paid for certain items, and <u>obsolete</u> material in the stockroom.

    A. overlooked   B. immoderate
    C. needed   D. instituted

11. Since <u>office</u> supplies are in such <u>common</u> use, an attitude of indifference about their handling is not <u>unusual</u>. Their importance is often recognized only when they are <u>utilized</u> or out of stock, for office employees must have proper supplies if maximum productivity is to be <u>attained</u>.

    A. plentiful   B. unavailable
    C. reduced   D. expected

12. Anyone <u>effected</u> by paperwork, <u>interested</u> in or engaged in office work, or desiring to improve <u>informational</u> activities can find materials <u>keyed</u> to his needs.

    A. attentive   B. available   C. affected   D. ambitious

13. Information is <u>homogeneous</u> and must therefore be properly classified so that each type may be <u>employed</u> in ways <u>appropriate</u> to its <u>own peculiar</u> properties.

    A. apparent   B. heterogeneous
    C. consistent   D. idiosyncratic

14. <u>Intellectual</u> training may seem a <u>formidable</u> phrase, but it means nothing more than the <u>deliberate</u> cultivation of the ability to think, and there is no <u>dark</u> contrast between the intellectual and the practical.

A. subjective   B. objective
C. sharp   D. vocational

15. The MOST important reason for having a filing system is to

    A. get papers out of the way
    B. have a record of everything that has happened
    C. retain information to justify your actions
    D. enable rapid retrieval of information

16. The system of filing which is used MOST frequently is called _____ filing.

    A. alphabetic   B. alphanumeric
    C. geographic   D. numeric

17. One of the clerks under your supervision has been telephoning frequently to tell you that he was taking the day off. Unless there is a real need for it, taking leave which is not scheduled is frowned upon because it upsets the work schedule.
    Under these circumstances, which of the following reasons for taking the day off is MOST acceptable?

    A. "I can't work when my arthritis bothers me."
    B. "I've been pressured with work from my night job and needed the extra time to catch up."
    C. "My family just moved to a new house, and I needed the time to start the repairs."
    D. "Work here has not been challenging, and I've been looking for another job."

18. One of the employees under your supervision, previously a very satisfactory worker, has begun arriving late one or two mornings each week. No explanation has been offered for this change. You call her to your office for a conference. As you are explaining the purpose of the conference and your need to understand this sudden lateness problem, she becomes angry and states that you have no right to question her.
    Of the following, the BEST course of action for you to take at this point is to

    A. inform her in your most authoritarian tone that you are the supervisor and that you have every right to question her
    B. end the conference and advise the employee that you will have no further discussion with her until she controls her temper
    C. remain calm, try to calm her down, and when she has quieted, explain the reasons for your questions and the need for answers
    D. hold your temper; when she has calmed down, tell her that you will not have a tardy worker in your unit and will have her transferred at once

19. Assume that, in the branch of the agency for which you work, you are the only clerical person on the staff with a supervisory title and, in addition, that you are the office manager. On a particular day when all members of the professional staff are away from the building attending an important meeting, an urgent call comes through requesting some confidential information ordinarily released only by professional staff.
    Of the following, the MOST reasonable action for you to take is to

    A. decline to give the information because you are not a member of the professional staff
    B. offer to call back after you get permission from the agency director at the main office

C. advise the caller that you will supply the information as soon as your chief returns
D. supply the information requested and inform your chief when she returns

20. As a supervisor, you are scheduled to attend an important conference with your superior. However, that day you learn that your very capable assistant is ill and unable to come to work. Several highly sensitive tasks are scheduled for completion on this day.
Of the following, the BEST way to handle this situation is to

   A. tell your supervisor you cannot attend the meeting and ask that it be postponed
   B. assign one of your staff to see that the jobs are completed and turned in
   C. advise your supervisor of the situation and ask what you should do
   D. call the departments for which the work is being done and ask for an extension of time

21. When a decision needs to be made which is likely to affect units other than his own, a supervisor should USUALLY

   A. make such a decision quickly and then discuss it with his supervisor
   B. make such a decision only after careful consultation with his subordinates
   C. discuss the problem with his immediate superior before making such a decision
   D. have his subordinates arrive at such a decision in conference with the subordinates in the other units

22. Assume that, as a supervisor in Division X, you are training Ms. Y, a new employee, to answer the telephone properly.
You should explain that the BEST way to answer is to pick up the receiver and say:

   A. "What is your name, please?"
   B. "May I help you?"
   C. "Ms. Y speaking."
   D. "Division X, Ms. Y speaking."

Questions 23-25.

DIRECTIONS: Questions 23 through 25 consist of sentences in which two words are missing. Examine each sentence, and then choose from below it the words which should be inserted in the blank spaces in order to create a coherent and well-written sentence.

23. Human behavior is far _____ variable, and therefore _____ predictable, than that of any other species.

   A. less; as
   B. less; not
   C. more; not
   D. more; less

24. The _____ limitation of this method is that the results are based _____ a narrow sample.

   A. chief; with
   B. chief; on
   C. only; for
   D. only; to

25. Although there _____ a standard procedure for handling these problems, each case often has _____ own unique features.

   A. are; its
   B. are; their
   C. is; its
   D. is; their

KEY (CORRECT ANSWERS)

1.	D		11.	B
2.	B		12.	C
3.	C		13.	B
4.	D		14.	C
5.	C		15.	D
6.	B		16.	A
7.	D		17.	A
8.	B		18.	C
9.	D		19.	B
10.	C		20.	C

21. C
22. D
23. D
24. B
25. C

———

TEST 2

DIRECTIONS: Each question or incomplete statement is followed by several suggested answers or completions. Select the one that BEST answers your question or completes the statement. *PRINT THE LETTER OF THE CORRECT ANSWER IN THE SPACE AT THE RIGHT.*

Questions 1-3.

DIRECTIONS: Questions 1 through 3 each consist of a group of four sentences. Read each sentence carefully, and select the one of the four in each group which represents the BEST English usage for business letters and reports.

1. A. The chairman himself, rather than his aides, hasreviewed the report.
    B. The chairman himself, rather than his aides, have reviewed the report.
    C. The chairmen, not the aide, has reviewed the report.
    D. The aide, not the chairmen, have reviewed the report.

2. A. Various proposals were submitted but the decision is not been made.
    B. Various proposals has been submitted but the decision has not been made.
    C. Various proposals were submitted but the decision is not been made.
    D. Various proposals have been submitted but the decision has not been made.

3. A. Everyone were rewarded for his successful attempt.
    B. They were successful in their attempts and each of them was rewarded.
    C. Each of them are rewarded for their successful attempts.
    D. The reward for their successful attempts were made to each of them.

4. Which of the following is MOST suited to arrangement in chronological order?

    A. Applications for various types and levels of jobs
    B. Issues of a weekly publication
    C. Weekly time cards for all employees for the week of April 21
    D. Personnel records for all employees

5. Words that are *synonymous* with a given word ALWAYS

    A. have the same meaning as the given word
    B. have the same pronunciation as the given word
    C. have the opposite meaning of the given word
    D. can be rhymed with the given word

Questions 6-11.

DIRECTIONS: Answer Questions 6 through 11 on the basis of the following chart showing numbers of errors made by four clerks in one work unit for a half-year period.

	Allan	Barry	Cary	David
July	5	4	1	7
Aug.	8	3	9	8
Sept.	7	8	7	5
Oct.	3	6	5	3
Nov.	2	4	4	6
Dec.	5	2	8	4

6. The clerk with the HIGHEST number of errors for the six-month period was

   A. Allan   B. Barry   C. Cary   D. David

7. If the number of errors made by Allan in the six months shown represented one-eighth of the total errors made by the unit during the entire year, what was the TOTAL number of errors made by the unit for the year?

   A. 124   B. 180   C. 240   D. 360

8. The number of errors made by David in November was what FRACTION of the total errors made in November?

   A. 1/3   B. 1/6   C. 3/8   D. 3/16

9. The average number of errors made per month per clerk was MOST NEARLY

   A. 4   B. 5   C. 6   D. 7

10. Of the total number of errors made during the six-month period, the percentage made in August was MOST NEARLY

    A. 2%   B. 4%   C. 23%   D. 44%

11. If the number of errors in the unit were to decrease in the next six months by 30%, what would be MOST NEARLY the total number of errors for the unit for the next six months?

    A. 87   B. 94   C. 120   D. 137

12. The arithmetic mean salary for five employees earning $18,500, $18,300, $18,600, $18,400, and $18,500, respectively, is

    A. $18,450   B. $18,460   C. $18,475   D. $18,500

13. Last year, a city department which is responsible for purchasing supplies ordered bond paper in equal quantities from 22 different companies. The price was exactly the same for each company, and the total cost for the 22 orders was $693,113.
    Assuming prices did not change during the year, the cost of EACH order was MOST NEARLY

    A. $31,490   B. $31,495   C. $31,500   D. $31,505

14. A city agency engaged in repair work uses a small part which the city purchases for 14? each. Assume that, in a certain year, the total expenditure of the city for this part was $700.
    How MANY of these parts were purchased that year?

    A. 50   B. 200   C. 2,000   D. 5,000

15. The work unit which you supervise is responsible for processing fifteen reports per month.
If your unit has four clerks and the best worker completes 40% of the reports himself, how many reports would each of the other clerks have to complete if they all do an equal number?

    A. 1 B. 2 C. 3 D. 4

16. Assume that the work unit in which you work has 24 clerks and 18 stenographers. In order to change the ratio of stenographers to clerks so that there is one stenographer for every four clerks, it would be necessary to REDUCE the number of stenographers by

    A. 3 B. 6 C. 9 D. 12

17. Assume that your office is responsible for opening and distributing all the mail of the division. After opening a letter, one of your subordinates notices that it states that there should be an enclosure in the envelope. However, there is no enclosure in the envelope. Of the following, the BEST instruction that you can give the clerk is to

    A. call the sender to obtain the enclosure
    B. call the addressee to inform him that the enclosure is missing
    C. note the omission in the margin of the letter
    D. forward the letter without taking any action

18. While opening the envelope containing official correspondence, you accidentally cut the enclosed letter.
Of the following, the BEST action for you to take is to

    A. leave the material as it is
    B. put it together by using transparent mending tape
    C. keep it together by putting it back in the envelope
    D. keep it together by using paper clips

19. Suppose your supervisor is on the telephone in his office and an applicant arrives for a scheduled interview with him.
Of the following, the BEST procedure to follow ordinarily is to

    A. informally chat with the applicant in your office until your supervisor has finished his phone conversation
    B. escort him directly into your supervisor's office and have him wait for him there
    C. inform your supervisor of the applicant's arrival and try to make the applicant feel comfortable while waiting
    D. have him hang up his coat and tell him to go directly in to see your supervisor

20. The length of time that files should be kept is GENERALLY

    A. considered to be seven years
    B. dependent upon how much new material has accumulated in the files
    C. directly proportionate to the number of years the office has been in operation
    D. dependent upon the type and nature of the material in the files

21. Cross-referencing a document when you file it means

   A. making a copy of the document and putting the copy into a related file
   B. indicating on the front of the document the name of the person who wrote it, the date it was written, and for what purpose
   C. putting a special sheet or card in a related file to indicate where the document is filed
   D. indicating on the document where it is to be filed

22. Unnecessary handling and recording of incoming mail could be eliminated by

   A. having the person who opens it initial it
   B. indicating on the piece of mail the names of all the individuals who should see it
   C. sending all incoming mail to more than one central location
   D. making a photocopy of each piece of incoming mail

23. Of the following, the office tasks which lend themselves MOST readily to planning and study are

   A. repetitive, occur in volume, and extend over a period of time
   B. cyclical in nature, have small volume, and extend over a short period of time
   C. tasks which occur only once in a great while not according to any schedule, and have large volume
   D. special tasks which occur only once, regardless of their volume and length of time

24. A good recordkeeping system includes all of the following procedures EXCEPT the

   A. filing of useless records
   B. destruction of certain files
   C. transferring of records from one type of file to another
   D. creation of inactive files

25. Assume that, as a supervisor, you are responsible for orienting and training new employees in your unit. Which of the following can MOST properly be omitted from your discussions with a new employee?

   A. The purpose of commonly used office forms
   B. Time and leave regulations
   C. Procedures for required handling of routine business calls
   D. The reason the last employee was fired

KEY (CORRECT ANSWERS)

1. A
2. D
3. B
4. B
5. A

6. C
7. C
8. C
9. B
10. C

11. A
12. B
13. D
14. D
15. C

16. D
17. C
18. B
19. C
20. D

21. C
22. B
23. A
24. A
25. D

READING COMPREHENSION
UNDERSTANDING AND INTERPRETING WRITTEN MATERIAL
EXAMINATION SECTION
TEST 1

DIRECTIONS: Each question or incomplete statement is followed by several suggested answers or completions. Select the one that BEST answers the question or completes the statement. *PRINT THE LETTER OF THE CORRECT ANSWER IN THE SPACE AT THE RIGHT.*

Questions 1-3.

DIRECTIONS: Questions 1 through 3 are to be answered SOLELY on the basis of the following statement.

The equipment in a mailroom may include a mail metering machine. This machine simultaneously stamps, postmarks, seals, and counts letters as fast as the operator can feed them. It can also print the proper postage directly on a gummed strip to be affixed to bulky items. It is equipped with a meter which is removed from the machine and sent to the postmaster to be set for a given number of stampings of any denomination. The setting of the meter must be paid for in advance. One of the advantages of metered mail is that it bypasses the cancellation operation and thereby facilitates handling by the post office. Mail metering also makes the pilfering of stamps impossible, but does not prevent the passage of personal mail in company envelopes through the meters unless there is established a rigid control or censorship over outgoing mail.

1. According to this statement, the postmaster

    A. is responsible for training new clerks in the use of mail metering machines
    B. usually recommends that both large and small firms adopt the use of mail metering machines
    C. is responsible for setting the meter to print a fixed number of stampings
    D. examines the mail metering machine to see that they are properly installed in the mailroom

2. According to this statement, the use of mail metering machines

    A. requires the employment of more clerks in a mailroom than does the use of postage stamps
    B. interferes with the handling of large quantities of outgoing mail
    C. does not prevent employees from sending their personal letters at company expense
    D. usually involves smaller expenditures for mailroom equipment than does the use of postage stamps

3. On the basis of this statement, it is MOST accurate to state that

    A. mail metering machines are often used for opening envelopes
    B. postage stamps are generally used when bulky packages are to be mailed
    C. the use of metered mail tends to interfere with rapid mail handling by the post office
    D. mail metering machines can seal and count letters at the same time

Questions 4-5.

DIRECTIONS: Questions 4 and 5 are to be answered SOLELY on the basis of the following statement.

Forms are printed sheets of paper on which information is to be entered. While what is printed on the form is most important, the kind of paper used in making the form is also important. The kind of paper should be selected with regard to the use to which the form will be subjected. Printing a form on an unnecessarily expensive grade of papers is wasteful. On the other hand, using too cheap or flimsy a form can materially interfere with satisfactory performance of the work the form is being planned to do. Thus, a form printed on both sides normally requires a heavier paper than a form printed only on one side. Forms to be used as permanent records, or which are expected to have a very long life in files, requires a quality of paper which will not disintegrate or discolor with age. A form which will go through a great deal of handling requires a strong, tough paper, while thinness is a necessary qualification where the making of several copies of a form will be required.

4. According to this statement, the type of paper used for making forms

   A. should be chosen in accordance with the use to which the form will be put
   B. should be chosen before the type of printing to be used has been decided upon
   C. is as important as the information which is printed on it
   D. should be strong enough to be used for any purpose

5. According to this statement, forms that are

   A. printed on both sides are usually economical and desirable
   B. to be filed permanently should not deteriorate as time goes on
   C. expected to last for a long time should be handled carefully
   D. to be filed should not be printed on inexpensive paper

Questions 6-8.

DIRECTIONS: Questions 6 through 8 are to be answered SOLELY on the basis of the following paragraph.

The increase in the number of public documents in the last two centuries closely matches the increase in population in the United States. The great number of public documents has become a serious threat to their usefulness. It is necessary to have programs which will reduce the number of public documents that are kept and which will, at the same time, assure keeping those that have value. Such programs need a great deal of thought to have any success.

6. According to the above paragraph, public documents may be LESS useful if

   A. the files are open to the public
   B. the record room is too small
   C. the copying machine is operated only during normal working hours
   D. too many records are being kept

7. According to the above paragraph, the growth of the population in the United States has matched the growth in the quantity of public documents for a period of MOST NEARLY _____ years.

   A. 50 B. 100 C. 200 D. 300

8. According to the above paragraph, the increased number of public documents has made it necessary to

   A. find out which public documents are worth keeping
   B. reduce the great number of public documents by decreasing government services
   C. eliminate the copying of all original public documents
   D. avoid all new copying devices

Questions 9-10.

DIRECTIONS: Questions 9 and 10 are to be answered SOLELY on the basis of the following paragraph.

The work goals of an agency can best be reached if the employees understand and agree with these goals. One way to gain such understanding and agreement is for management to encourage and seriously consider suggestions from employees in the setting of agency goals.

9. On the basis of the above paragraph, the BEST way to achieve the work goals of an agency is to

   A. make certain that employees work as hard as possible
   B. study the organizational structure of the agency
   C. encourage employees to think seriously about the agency's problems
   D. stimulate employee understanding of the work goals

10. On the basis of the above paragraph, understanding and agreement with agency goals can be gained by

    A. allowing the employees to set agency goals
    B. reaching agency goals quickly
    C. legislative review of agency operations
    D. employee participation in setting agency goals

Questions 11-13.

DIRECTIONS: Questions 11 through 13 are to be answered SOLELY on the basis of the following paragraph.

In order to organize records properly, it is necessary to start from their very beginning and trace each copy of the record to find out how it is used, how long it is used, and what may finally be done with it. Although several copies of the record are made, one copy should be marked as the copy of record. This is the formal legal copy, held to meet the requirements of the law. The other copies may be retained for brief periods for reference purposes, but these copies should not be kept after their usefulness as reference ends. There is another reason for tracing records through the office and that is to determine how long it takes the copy of record to reach the central file. The copy of record must not be kept longer than necessary by the section of the office which has prepared it, but should be sent to the central file as soon as possible so that it can be available to the various sections of the office. The central file can make the copy of record available to the various sections of the office at an early date only if it arrives at the central file as quickly as possible. Just as soon as its immediate or active service period is ended, the copy of record should be removed from the central file and put into the inactive file in the office to be stored for whatever length of time may be necessary to meet legal requirements, and then destroyed.

11. According to the above paragraph, a reason for tracing records through an office is to

    A. determine how long the central file must keep the records
    B. organize records properly
    C. find out how many copies of each record are required
    D. identify the copy of record

12. According to the above paragraph, in order for the central file to have the copy of record available as soon as possible for the various sections of the office, it is MOST important that the

    A. copy of record to be sent to the central file meets the requirements of the law
    B. copy of record is not kept in the inactive file too long
    C. section preparing the copy of record does not unduly delay in sending it to the central file
    D. central file does not keep the copy of record beyond its active service period

13. According to the above paragraph, the length of time a copy of a record is kept in the inactive file of an office depends CHIEFLY on the

    A. requirements of the law
    B. length of time that is required to trace the copy of record through the office
    C. use that is made of the copy of record
    D. length of the period that the copy of record is used for reference purposes

Questions 14-16.

DIRECTIONS: Questions 14 through 16 are to be answered SOLELY on the basis of the following paragraph.

The office was once considered as nothing more than a focal point of internal and external correspondence. It was capable only of dispatching a few letters upon occasion and of preparing records of little practical value. Under such a concept, the vitality of the office force was impaired. Initiative became stagnant, and the lot of the office worker was not likely to be a happy one. However, under the new concept of office management, the possibilities of waste and mismanagement in office operation are now fully recognized, as are the possibilities for the modern office to assist in the direction and control of business operations. Fortunately, the modern concept of the office as a centralized service-rendering unit is gaining ever greater acceptance in today's complex business world, for without the modern office, the production wheels do not turn and the distribution of goods and services is not possible.

14. According to the above paragraph, the fundamental difference between the old and the new concept of the office is the change in the

    A. accepted functions of the office
    B. content and the value of the records kept
    C. office methods and systems
    D. vitality and morale of the office force

15. According to the above paragraph, an office operated today under the old concept of the office MOST likely would

    A. make older workers happy in their jobs
    B. be part of an old thriving business concern
    C. have a passive role in the conduct of a business enterprise
    D. attract workers who do not believe in modern methods

16. Of the following, the MOST important implication of the above paragraph is that a present-day business organization cannot function effectively without the

    A. use of modern office equipment
    B. participation and cooperation of the office
    C. continued modernization of office procedures
    D. employment of office workers with skill and initiative

Questions 17-20.

DIRECTIONS: Questions 17 through 20 are to be answered SOLELY on the basis of the following paragraph.

A report is frequently ineffective because the person writing it is not fully acquainted with all the necessary details before he actually starts to construct the report. All details pertaining to the subject should be known before the report is started. If the essential facts are not known, they should be investigated. It is wise to have essential facts written down rather than to depend too much on memory, especially if the facts pertain to such matters as amounts, dates, names of persons, or other specific data. When the necessary information has been gathered, the general plan and content of the report should be thought out before the writing is actually begun. A person with little or no experience in writing reports may find that it is wise to make a brief outline. Persons with more experience should not need a written outline, but they should make mental notes of the steps they are to follow. If writing reports without dictation is a regular part of an office worker's duties, he should set aside a certain time during the day when he is least likely to be interrupted. That may be difficult, but in most offices there are certain times in the day when the callers, telephone calls, and other interruptions are not numerous. During those times, it is best to write reports that need undivided concentration. Reports that are written amid a series of interruptions may be poorly done.

17. Before starting to write an effective report, it is necessary to

    A. memorize all specific information
    B. disregard ambiguous data
    C. know all pertinent information
    D. develop a general plan

6 (#1)

18. Reports dealing with complex and difficult material should be

   A. prepared and written by the supervisor of the unit
   B. written when there is the least chance of interruption
   C. prepared and written as part of regular office routine
   D. outlined and then dictated

18.____

19. According to the paragraph, employees with no prior familiarity in writing reports may find it helpful to

   A. prepare a brief outline
   B. mentally prepare a synopsis of the report's content
   C. have a fellow employee help in writing the report
   D. consult previous reports

19.____

20. In writing a report, needed information which is unclear should be

   A. disregarded   B. memorized
   C. investigated   D. gathered

20.____

Questions 21-25.

DIRECTIONS: Questions 21 through 25 are to be answered SOLELY on the basis of the following passage.

   Positive discipline minimizes the amount of personal supervision required and aids in the maintenance of standards. When a new employee has been properly introduced and carefully instructed, when he has come to know the supervisor and has confidence in the supervisor's ability to take care of him, when he willingly cooperates with the supervisor, that employee has been under positive discipline and can be put on his own to produce the quantity and quality of work desired. Negative discipline, the fear of transfer to a less desirable location, for example, to a limited extent may restrain certain individuals from overt violation of rules and regulations governing attendance and conduct which in governmental agencies are usually on at least an agency-wide basis. Negative discipline may prompt employees to perform according to certain rules to avoid a penalty such as, for example, docking for tardiness.

21. According to the above passage, it is reasonable to assume that in the area of discipline, the first-line supervisor in a governmental agency has GREATER scope for action in

   A. *positive* discipline, because negative discipline is largely taken care of by agency rules and regulations
   B. *negative* discipline, because rules and procedures are already fixed and the supervisor can rely on them
   C. *positive* discipline, because the supervisor is in a position to recommend transfers
   D. *negative* discipline, because positive discipline is reserved for people on a higher supervisory level

21.____

22. In order to maintain positive discipline of employees under his supervision, it is MOST important for a supervisor to

   A. assure each employee that he has nothing to worry about
   B. insist at the outset on complete cooperation from employees

22.____

C. be sure that each employee is well trained in his job
D. inform new employees of the penalties for not meeting standards

23. According to the above passage, a feature of negative discipline is that it   23.____

    A. may lower employee morale
    B. may restrain employees from disobeying the rules
    C. censures equal treatment of employees
    D. tends to create standards for quality of work

24. A REASONABLE conclusion based on the above passage is that positive discipline benefits a supervisor because   24.____

    A. he can turn over orientation and supervision of a new employee to one of his subordinates
    B. subordinates learn to cooperate with one another when working on an assignment
    C. it is easier to administer
    D. it cuts down, in the long run, on the amount of time the supervisor needs to spend on direct supervision

25. Based on the above passage, it is REASONABLE to assume, that an important difference between positive discipline and negative discipline is that positive discipline   25.____

    A. is concerned with the quality of work and negative discipline with the quantity of work
    B. leads to a more desirable basis for motivation of the employee
    C. is more likely to be concerned with agency rules and regulations
    D. uses fear while negative discipline uses penalties to prod employees to adequate performance

KEY (CORRECT ANSWERS)

1.	C	11.	B
2.	C	12.	C
3.	D	13.	A
4.	A	14.	A
5.	B	15.	C
6.	D	16.	B
7.	C	17.	C
8.	A	18.	B
9.	D	19.	A
10.	D	20.	B

21. A
22. C
23. B
24. D
25. B

TEST 2

Questions 1-6.

DIRECTIONS: Questions 1 through 6 are to be answered SOLELY on the basis of the following passage.

Inherent in all organized endeavors is the need to resolve the individual differences involved in conflict. Conflict may be either a positive or negative factor since it may lead to creativity, innovation and progress on the one hand, or it may result, on the other hand, in a deterioration or even destruction of the organization. Thus, some forms of conflict are desirable, whereas others are undesirable and ethically wrong.

There are three management strategies which deal with interpersonal conflict. In the *divide-and-rule strategy,* management attempts to maintain control by limiting the conflict to those directly involved and preventing their disagreement from spreading to the larger group. The *suppression-of-differences strategy* entails ignoring conflicts or pretending they are irrelevant. In the *working-through-differences strategy,* management actively attempts to solve or resolve intergroup or interpersonal conflicts. Of the three strategies, only the last directly attacks and has the potential for eliminating the causes of conflict. An essential part of this strategy, however, is its employment by a committed and relatively mature management team.

1. According to the above passage, the *divide-and-rule strategy tor* dealing with conflict is the attempt to

    A. involve other people in the conflict
    B. restrict the conflict to those participating in it
    C. divide the conflict into positive and negative factors
    D. divide the conflict into a number of smaller ones

2. The word *conflict* is used in relation to both positive and negative factors in this passage. Which one of the following words is MOST likely to describe the activity which the word *conflict,* in the sense of the passage, implies?

    A. Competition   B. Confusion
    C. Cooperation   D. Aggression

3. According to the above passage, which one of the following characteristics is shared by both the *suppression-of-differences strategy* and the *divide-and-rule strategy*?

    A. Pretending that conflicts are irrelevant
    B. Preventing conflicts from spreading to the group situation
    C. Failure to directly attack the causes of conflict
    D. Actively attempting to resolve interpersonal conflict

4. According to the above passage, the successful resolution of interpersonal conflict requires

    A. allowing the group to mediate conflicts between two individuals
    B. division of the conflict into positive and negative factors
    C. involvement of a committed, mature management team
    D. ignoring minor conflicts until they threaten the organization

5. Which can be MOST reasonably inferred from the above passage? Conflict between two individuals is LEAST likely to continue when management uses

   A. the *working-through differences strategy*
   B. the *suppression-of differences strategy*
   C. the *divide-and-rule strategy*
   D. a combination of all three strategies

6. According to the above passage, a DESIRABLE result of conflict in an organization is when conflict

   A. exposes production problems in the organization
   B. can be easily ignored by management
   C. results in advancement of more efficient managers
   D. leads to development of new methods

Questions 7-13.

DIRECTIONS: Questions 7 through 13 are to be answered SOLELY on the basis of the passage below.

Modern management places great emphasis on the concept of communication. The communication process consists of the steps through which an idea or concept passes from its inception by one person, the sender, until it is acted upon by another person, the receiver. Through an understanding of these steps and some of the possible barriers that may occur, more effective communication may be achieved. The first step in the communication process is ideation by the sender. This is the formation of the intended content of the message he wants to transmit. In the next step, encoding, the sender organizes his ideas into a series of symbols designed to communicate his message to his intended receiver. He selects suitable words or phrases that can be understood by the receiver, and he also selects the appropriate media to be used—for example, memorandum, conference, etc. The third step is transmission of the encoded message through selected channels in the organizational structure. In the fourth step, the receiver enters the process by tuning in to receive the message. If the receiver does not function, however, the message is lost. For example, if the message is oral, the receiver must be a good listener. The fifth step is decoding of the message by the receiver, as for example, by changing words into ideas. At this step, the decoded message may not be the same idea that the sender originally encoded because the sender and receiver have different perceptions regarding the meaning of certain words. Finally, the receiver acts or responds. He may file the information, ask for more information, or take other action. There can be no assurance, however, that communication has taken place unless there is some type of feedback to the sender in the form of an acknowledgement that the message was received.

7. According to the above passage, *ideation* is the process by which the

   A. sender develops the intended content of the message
   B. sender organizes his ideas into a series of symbols
   C. receiver tunes in to receive the message
   D. receiver decodes the message

8. In the last sentence of the passage, the word *feedback* refers to the process by which the sender is assured that the

    A. receiver filed the information
    B. receiver's perception is the same as his own
    C. message was received
    D. message was properly interpreted

9. Which one of the following BEST shows the order of the steps in the communication process as described in the passage?

    A. 1 - ideation   2 - encoding
        3 - decoding   4 - transmission
        5 - receiving   6 - action
        7 - feedback to the sender

    B. 1 - ideation   2 - encoding
        3 - transmission   4 - decoding
        5 - receiving   6 - action
        7 - feedback to the sender

    C. 1 - ideation   2 - decoding
        3 - transmission   4 - receiving
        5 - encoding   6 - action
        7 - feedback to the sender

    D. 1 - ideation   2 - encoding
        3 - transmission   4 - receiving
        5 - decoding   6 - action
        7 - feedback to the sender

10. Which one of the following BEST expresses the main theme of the passage?

    A. Different individuals have the same perceptions regarding the meaning of words.
    B. An understanding of the steps in the communication process may achieve better communication.
    C. Receivers play a passive role in the communication process.
    D. Senders should not communicate with receivers who transmit feedback.

11. The above passage implies that a receiver does NOT function properly when he

    A. transmits feedback   B. files the information
    C. is a poor listener   D. asks for more information

12. Which one of the following, according to the above passage, is included in the SECOND step of the communication process?

    A. Selecting the appropriate media to be used in transmission
    B. Formulation of the intended content of the message
    C. Using appropriate media to respond to the receiver's feedback
    D. Transmitting the message through selected channels in the organization

13. The above passage implies that the *decoding process* is MOST NEARLY the reverse of the _____ process.

    A. transmission   B. receiving
    C. feedback   D. encoding

Questions 14-19.

DIRECTIONS: Questions 14 through 19 are to be answered SOLELY on the basis of the following passage.

It is often said that no system will work if the people who carry it out do not want it to work. In too many cases, a departmental reorganization that seemed technically sound and economically practical has proved to be a failure because the planners neglected to take the human factor into account. The truth is that employees are likely to feel threatened when they learn that a major change is in the wind. It does not matter whether or not the change actually poses a threat to an employee; the fact that he believes it does or fears it might is enough to make him feel insecure. Among the dangers he fears, the foremost is the possibility that his job may cease to exist and that he may be laid off or shunted into a less skilled position at lower pay. Even if he knows that his own job category is secure, however, he is likely to fear losing some of the important intangible advantages of his present position—for instance, he may fear that he will be separated from his present companions and thrust in with a group of strangers, or that he will find himself in a lower position on the organizational ladder if a new position is created above his.

It is important that management recognize these natural fears and take them into account in planning any kind of major change. While there is no cut-and-dried formula for preventing employee resistance, there are several steps that can be taken to reduce employees' fears and gain their cooperation. First, unwarranted fears can be dispelled if employees are kept informed of the planning from the start and if they know exactly what to expect. Next, assurance on matters such as retraining, transfers, and placement help should be given as soon as it is clear what direction the reorganization will take. Finally, employees' participation in the planning should be actively sought. There is a great psychological difference between feeling that a change is being forced upon one from the outside, and feeling that one is an insider who is helping to bring about a change.

14. According to the above passage, employees who are not in real danger of losing their jobs because of a proposed reorganization

    A. will be eager to assist in the reorganization
    B. will pay little attention to the reorganization
    C. should not be taken into account in planning the reorganization
    D. are nonetheless likely to feel threatened by the reorganization

14.____

15. The passage mentions the *intangible advantages* of a position.
Which of the following BEST describes the kind of advantages alluded to in the passage?

    A. Benefits such as paid holidays and vacations
    B. Satisfaction of human needs for things like friendship and status
    C. Qualities such as leadership and responsibility
    D. A work environment that meets satisfactory standards of health and safety

15.____

16. According to the passage, an employee's fear that a reorganization may separate him from his present companions is a (n)

    A. childish and immature reaction to change
    B. unrealistic feeling since this is not going to happen

16.____

C. possible reaction that the planners should be aware of
D. incentive to employees to participate in the planning

17. On the basis of the above passage, it would be DESIRABLE, when planning a departmental reorganization, to

   A. be governed by employee feelings and attitudes
   B. give some employees lower positions
   C. keep employees informed
   D. lay off those who are less skilled

18. What does the passage say can be done to help gain employees' cooperation in a reorganization?

   A. Making sure that the change is technically sound, that it is economically practical, and that the human factor is taken into account
   B. Keeping employees fully informed, offering help in fitting them into new positions, and seeking their participation in the planning
   C. Assuring employees that they will not be laid off, that they will not be reassigned to a group of strangers, and that no new positions will be created on the organization ladder
   D. Reducing employees' fears, arranging a retraining program, and providing for transfers

19. Which of the following suggested titles would be MOST appropriate for this passage?

   A. PLANNING A DEPARTMENTAL REORGANIZATION
   B. WHY EMPLOYEES ARE AFRAID
   C. LOOKING AHEAD TO THE FUTURE
   D. PLANNING FOR CHANGE: THE HUMAN FACTOR

Questions 20-22.

DIRECTIONS: Questions 20 through 22 are to be answered SOLELY on the basis of the following passage.

The achievement of good human relations is essential if a business office is to produce at top efficiency and is to be a pleasant place in which to work. All office workers plan an important role in handling problems in human relations. They should, therefore, strive to acquire the understanding, tactfulness, and awareness necessary to deal effectively with actual office situations involving co-workers on all levels. Only in this way can they truly become responsible, interested, cooperative, and helpful members of the staff.

20. The selection implies that the MOST important value of good human relations in an office is to develop

   A. efficiency   B. cooperativeness
   C. tact   D. pleasantness and efficiency

21. Office workers should acquire understanding in dealing with

   A. co-workers   B. subordinates
   C. superiors   D. all members of the staff

22. The selection indicates that a highly competent secretary who is also very argumentative is meeting office requirements

    A. wholly
    B. partly
    C. slightly
    D. not at all

Questions 23-25.

DIRECTIONS: Questions 23 through 25 are to be answered SOLELY on the basis of the following passage.

It is common knowledge that ability to do a particular job and performance on the job do not always go hand in hand. Persons with great potential abilities sometimes fall down on the job because of laziness or lack of interest in the job, while persons with mediocre talents have often achieved excellent results through their industry and their loyalty to the interests of their employers. It is clear; therefore, that in a balanced personnel program, measures of employee ability need to be supplemented by measures of employee performance, for the final test of any employee is his performance on the job.

23. The MOST accurate of the following statements, on the basis of the above paragraph, is that

    A. employees who lack ability are usually not industrious
    B. an employee's attitudes are more important than his abilities
    C. mediocre employees who are interested in their work are preferable to employees who possess great ability
    D. superior capacity for performance should be supplemented with proper attitudes

24. On the basis of the above paragraph, the employee of most value to his employer is NOT necessarily the one who

    A. best understands the significance of his duties
    B. achieves excellent results
    C. possesses the greatest talents
    D. produces the greatest amount of work

25. According to the above paragraph, an employee's efficiency is BEST determined by an

    A. appraisal of his interest in his work
    B. evaluation of the work performed by him
    C. appraisal of his loyalty to his employer
    D. evaluation of his potential ability to perform his work

KEY (CORRECT ANSWERS)

1.	B	11.	C
2.	A	12.	A
3.	C	13.	D
4.	C	14.	D
5.	A	15.	B
6.	D	16.	C
7.	A	17.	C
8.	C	18.	B
9.	D	19.	D
10.	B	20.	D

21. D
22. B
23. D
24. C
25. B

TEST 3

Questions 1-8.

DIRECTIONS: Questions 1 through 8 are to be answered SOLELY on the basis of the following information and directions.

Assume that you are a clerk in a city agency. Your supervisor has asked you to classify each of the accidents that happened to employees in the agency into the following five categories:

A. An accident that occurred in the period from January through June, between 9 A.M. and 12 Noon, that was the result of carelessness on the part of the injured employee, that caused the employee to lose less than seven working hours, that happened to an employee who was 40 years of age or over, and who was employed in the agency for less than three years;

B. An accident that occurred in the period from July through December, after 1 P.M., that was the result of unsafe conditions, that caused the injured employee to lose less than seven working hours, that happened to an employee who was 40 years of age or over, and who was employed in the agency for three years or more;

C. An accident that occurred in the period from January through June, after 1 P.M., that was the result of carelessness on the part of the injured employee, that caused the injured employee to lose seven or more working hours, that happened to an employee who was less than 40 years old, and who was employed in the agency for three years or more;

D. An accident that occurred in the period from July through December, between 9 A.M. and 12 Noon, that was the result of unsafe conditions, that caused the injured employee to lose seven or more working hours, that happened to an employee who was less than 40 years old, and who was employed in the agency for less than three years;

E. Accidents that cannot be classified in any of the foregoing groups. NOTE: In classifying these accidents, an employee's age and length of service are computed as of the date of accident. In all cases, it is to be assumed that each employee has been employed continuously in city service, and that each employee works seven hours a day, from 9 A.M. to 5 P.M., with lunch from 12 Noon to 1 P.M. In each question, consider only the information which will assist you in classifying the accident. Any information which is of no assistance in classifying an accident should not be considered.

1. The unsafe condition of the stairs in the building caused Miss Perkins to have an accident on October 14, 2003 at 4 P.M. When she returned to work the following day at 1 P.M., Miss Perkins said that the accident was the first one that had occurred to her in her ten years of employment with the agency. She was born on April 27, 1962.

2. On the day after she completed her six-month probationary period of employment with the agency, Miss Green, who had been considered a careful worker by her supervisor, injured her left foot in an accident caused by her own carelessness. She went home immediately after the accident, which occurred at 10 A.M., March 19, 2004, but returned to work at the regular time on the following morning. Miss Green was born July 12, 1963 in New York City.

3. The unsafe condition of a duplicating machine caused Mr. Martin to injure himself in an accident on September 8, 2006 at 2 P.M. As a result of the accident, he was unable to work the remainder of the day, but returned to his office ready for work on the following morning. Mr. Martin, who has been working for the agency since April 1, 2003, was born in St. Louis on February 1, 1968.

3.____

4. Mr. Smith was hospitalized for two weeks because of a back injury resulted from an accident on the morning of November 16, 2006. Investigation of the accident revealed that it was caused by the unsafe condition of the floor on which Mr. Smith had been walking. Mr. Smith, who is an accountant, has been an employee of the agency since March 1, 2004, and was born in Ohio on June 10, 1968.

4.____

5. Mr. Allen cut his right hand because he was careless in operating a multilith machine. Mr. Allen, who was 33 years old when the accident took place, has been employed by the agency since August 17, 1992. The accident, which occurred on January 26, 2006, at 2 P.M., caused Mr. Allen to be absent from work for the rest of the day. He was able to return to work the next morning.

5.____

6. Mr. Rand, who is a college graduate, was born on December, 28, 1967, and has been working for the agency since January 7, 2002. On Monday, April 25, 2005, at 2 P.M., his carelessness in operating a duplicating machine caused him to have an accident and to be sent home from work immediately. Fortunately, he was able to return to work at his regular time on the following Wednesday.

6.____

7. Because he was careless in running down a flight of stairs, Mr. Brown fell, bruising his right hand. Although the accident occurred shortly after he arrived for work on the morning of May 22, 2006, he was unable to resume work until 3 P.M. that day. Mr. Brown was born on August 15, 1955, and began working for the agency on September 12, 2003, as a clerk, at a salary of $22,750 per annum.

7.____

8. On December 5, 2005, four weeks after he had begun working for the agency, the unsafe condition of an automatic stapling machine caused Mr. Thomas to injure himself in an accident. Mr. Thomas, who was born on May 19, 1975, lost three working days because of the accident, which occurred at 11:45 A.M.

8.____

Questions 9-10.

DIRECTIONS: Questions 9 and 10 are to be answered SOLELY on the basis of the following paragraph.

An impending reorganization within an agency will mean loss by transfer of several professional staff members from the personnel division. The division chief is asked to designate the persons to be transferred. After reviewing the implications of this reduction of staff with his assistant, the division chief discusses the matter at a staff meeting. He adopts the recommendations of several staff members to have volunteers make up the required reduction.

9. The decision to permit personnel to volunteer for transfer is

   A. *poor;* it is not likely that the members of a division are of equal value to the division chief
   B. *good;* dissatisfied members will probably be more productive elsewhere
   C. *poor;* the division chief has abdicated his responsibility to carry out the order given to him
   D. *good;* morale among remaining staff is likely to improve in a more cohesive framework

10. Suppose that one of the volunteers is a recently appointed employee who has completed his probationary period acceptably, but whose attitude toward division operations and agency administration tends to be rather negative and sometimes even abrasive. Because of his lack of commitment to the division, his transfer is recommended. If the transfer is approved, the division chief should, prior to the transfer,

    A. discuss with the staff the importance of commitment to the work of the agency and its relationship with job satisfaction
    B. refrain from any discussion of attitude with the employee
    C. discuss with the employee his concern about the employee's attitude
    D. avoid mention of attitude in the evaluation appraisal prepared for the receiving division chief

Questions 11-16.

DIRECTIONS: Questions 11 through 16 are to be answered SOLELY on the basis of the following paragraph.

Methods of administration of office activities, much of which consists of providing information and *know-how* needed to coordinate both activities within that particular office and other offices, have been among the last to come under the spotlight of management analysis. Progress has been rapid during the past decade, however, and is now accelerating at such a pace that an *information revolution* in office management appears to be in the making. Although triggered by technological breakthroughs in electronic computers and other giant steps in mechanization, this information revolution must be attributed to underlying forces, such as the increased complexity of both governmental and private enterprise, and ever-keener competition. Size, diversification, specialization of function, and decentralization are among the forces which make coordination of activities both more imperative and more difficult. Increased competition, both domestic and international, leaves little margin for error in managerial decisions. Several developments during recent years indicate an evolving pattern. In 1960, the American Management Association expanded the scope of its activities and changed the name of its Office Management Division to Administrative Services Division. Also in 1960, the magazine *Office Management* merged with the magazine *American Business,* and this new publication was named *Administrative Management.*

11. A REASONABLE inference that can be made from the information in the above paragraph is that an important role of the office manager today is to

    A. work toward specialization of functions performed by his subordinates
    B. inform and train subordinates regarding any new developments in computer technology and mechanization
    C. assist the professional management analysts with the management analysis work in the organization
    D. supply information that can be used to help coordinate and manage the other activities of the organization

12. An IMPORTANT reason for the *information revolution* that has been taking place in office management is the

    A. advance made in management analysis in the past decade
    B. technological breakthrough in electronic computers and mechanization
    C. more competitive and complicated nature of private business and government
    D. increased efficiency of office management techniques in the past ten years

13. According to the above paragraph, specialization of function in an organization is MOST likely to result in

    A. the elimination of errors in managerial decisions
    B. greater need to coordinate activities
    C. more competition with other organizations, both domestic and international
    D. a need for office managers with greater flexibility

14. The word *evolving,* as used in the third from last sentence in the above paragraph, means MOST NEARLY

    A. developing by gradual changes
    B. passing on to others
    C. occurring periodically
    D. breaking up into separate, constituent parts

15. Of the following, the MOST reasonable implication of the changes in names mentioned in the last part of the above paragraph is that these groups are attempting to

    A. professionalize the field of office management and the title of Office Manager
    B. combine two publications into one because of the increased costs of labor and materials
    C. adjust to the fact that the field of office management is broadening
    D. appeal to the top managerial people rather than the office management people in business and government

16. According to the above paragraph, intense competition among domestic and international enterprises makes it MOST important for an organization's managerial staff to

    A. coordinate and administer office activities with other activities in the organization
    B. make as few errors in decision-making as possible
    C. concentrate on decentralization and reduction of size of the individual divisions of the organization
    D. restrict decision-making only to top management officials

Questions 17-21.

DIRECTIONS: Questions 17 through 21 are to be answered SOLELY on the basis of the following passage.

For some office workers, it is useful to be familiar with the four main classes of domestic mail; for others, it is essential. Each class has a different rate of postage, and some have requirements concerning wrapping, sealing, or special information to be placed on the package. First class mail, the class which may not be opened for postal inspection, includes letters, postcards, business reply cards, and other kinds of written matter. There are different rates for some of the kinds of cards which can be sent by first class mail. The maximum weight for an item sent by first class mail is 70 pounds. An item which is not letter size should be marked *First Class* on all sides. Although office workers most often come into contact with first class mail, they may find it helpful to know something about the other classes. Second class mail is generally used for mailing newspapers and magazines. Publishers of these articles must meet certain U.S. Postal Service requirements in order to obtain a permit to use second class mailing rates. Third class mail, which must weigh less than 1 pound, includes printed materials and merchandise parcels. There are two rate structures for this class - a single piece rate and a bulk rate. Fourth class mail, also known as parcel post, includes packages weighing from one to 40 pounds. For more information about these classes of mail and the actual mailing rates, contact your local post office.

17. According to this passage, first class mail is the *only* class which

    A. has a limit on the maximum weight of an item
    B. has different rates for items within the class
    C. may not be opened for postal inspection
    D. should be used by office workers

18. According to this passage, the one of the following items which may CORRECTLY be sent by fourth class mail is a

    A. magazine weighing one-half pound
    B. package weighing one-half pound
    C. package weighing two pounds
    D. postcard

19. According to this passage, there are different postage rates for

    A. a newspaper sent by second class mail and a magazine sent by second class mail
    B. each of the classes of mail
    C. each pound of fourth class mail
    D. printed material sent by third class mail and merchandise parcels sent by third class mail

20. In order to send a newspaper by second class mail, a publisher MUST

    A. have met certain postal requirements and obtained a permit
    B. indicate whether he wants to use the single piece or the bulk rate
    C. make certain that the newspaper weighs less than one pound
    D. mark the newspaper *Second Class* on the top and bottom of the wrapper

21. Of the following types of information, the one which is NOT mentioned in the passage is the 21.____

    A. class of mail to which parcel post belongs
    B. kinds of items which can be sent by each class of mail
    C. maximum weight for an item sent by fourth class mail
    D. postage rate for each of the four classes of mail

Questions 22-25.

DIRECTIONS: Questions 22 through 25 are to be answered SOLELY on the basis of the following paragraph.

A standard comprises characteristics attached to an aspect of a process or product by which it can be evaluated. Standardization is the development and adoption of standards. When they are formulated, standards are not usually the product of a single person, but represent the thoughts and ideas of a group, leavened with the knowledge and information which are currently available. Standards which do not meet certain basic requirements become a hindrance rather than an aid to progress. Standards must not only be correct, accurate, and precise in requiring no more and no less than what is needed for satisfactory results, but they must also be workable in the sense that their usefulness is not nullified by external conditions. Standards should also be acceptable to the people who use them. If they are not acceptable, they cannot be considered to be satisfactory, although they may possess all the other essential characteristics.

22. According to the above paragraph, a processing standard that requires the use of materials that cannot be procured is MOST likely to be 22.____

    A. incomplete   B. unworkable
    C. inaccurate   D. unacceptable

23. According to the above paragraph, the construction of standards to which the performance of job duties should conform is MOST often 23.____

    A. the work of the people responsible for seeing that the duties are properly performed
    B. accomplished by the person who is best informed about the functions involved
    C. the responsibility of the people who are to apply them
    D. attributable to the efforts of various informed persons

24. According to the above paragraph, when standards call for finer tolerances than those essential to the conduct of successful production operations, the effect of the standards on the improvement of production operations is 24.____

    A. negative   B. negligible
    C. nullified   D. beneficial

25. The one of the following which is the MOST suitable title for the above paragraph is 25.____

    A. THE EVALUATION OF FORMULATED STANDARDS
    B. THE ATTRIBUTES OF SATISFACTORY STANDARDS
    C. THE ADOPTION OF ACCEPTABLE STANDARDS
    D. THE USE OF PROCESS OR PRODUCT STANDARDS

KEY (CORRECT ANSWERS)

1.	B		11.	D
2.	A		12.	C
3.	E		13.	B
4.	D		14.	A
5.	E		15.	C
6.	C		16.	B
7.	A		17.	C
8.	D		18.	C
9.	A		19.	B
10.	C		20.	A

21. D
22. C
23. D
24. A
25. B